BLUE NOSE
JUSTICE

True tales of mischief, mayhem and murder

Dean Jobb

Pottersfield Press, Lawrencetown Beach,
Nova Scotia, Canada
1993

This book is dedicated to Pat Duncan and Mike
Lambert, great lawyers and great friends.

Canadian Cataloguing in Publication
Jobb, Dean, 1958-

Bluenose justice

ISBN 0-919001-78-5

1. Crime -- Nova Scotia -- History. 2. Criminals -- Nova Scotia
--History. 3. Criminal justice, Administration of -- Nova Scotia.
I. Title.

HV6809.N6J6 1993   364.9716'09   C93-098604-0

Published with the financial support of the Nova Scotia Department of Tourism and Culture, the Canada Council and the
Department of Communications.

Pottersfield Press
Lawrencetown Beach
R.R. 2, Porters Lake
Nova Scotia B0J 2S0

Contents

by a one-way trip to the gallows. A brief history of the noose in Nova Scotia.

It didn't take long for Halifax to witness its first murder after the city was founded in 1749. It didn't take long for justice to run its course, either.

It's been two centuries since George and John Boutilier were tried for a triple murder in Lunenburg. Their guilt or innocence turned on a single shred of evidence.

Part Six
MURDER MOST FOUL

The brutal death of a penniless woman shocked Victorian Nova Scotia. But it would take the province's best prosecutor to nail the villain.

It was almost the perfect crime — leave no witnesses, make a fast getaway. There was still one loose end — how did Maurice Doyle wind up with a dead man's wallet?

James Robinson Johnston could have been the first Nova Scotia Black to win elected office, and maybe even the province's first black judge. But his promising career was tragically cut short in 1915.

Introduction

*Wherever there is authority, there is a natural
inclination to disobedience.*
— Thomas Chandler Haliburton, 1853.

Rumrunner Jack Randell, who flouted the prohibition laws, no doubt would agree with that observation by Haliburton, the great Nova Scotia satirist. So would Joseph Howe, the crusading Halifax editor who used his newspaper and the courtroom to expose government corruption in the 1830s. But that's about all Randell and Howe would agree on. Howe challenged the authority of government officials who were more interested in lining their own pockets than in furthering the public good. A century later, Randell seized the chance to turn a fast buck by smuggling booze into the United States. Randell's brush with authority — in the form of the U.S. Coast Guard — sparked an international incident, cost him his ship, and nearly cost him his life.

Howe and Randell may have approached authority with differing motives, but they proved Haliburton's point. Laws, good or bad, are made to be broken. And the authority that creates or enforces those laws will always have to deal with those inclined to disobey. As this book shows, Nova Scotia has had no shortage of people willing to break the law or to use it to serve their own ends.

Bluenose Justice is a collection of more than a dozen stories about crime and criminals, lawyers and litigants, judges and justice, drawn from roughly two centuries of Nova Scotia's history. The events occurred in Sydney, Lunenburg, Amherst, Annapolis Royal and points in between. But the characters who inhabit these pages have an appeal that extends beyond Nova Scotia's borders and into the present day. And the themes that run through these stories — greed, vengeance, or simply the quest for justice — are universal.

For a lesson in the evils of greed, look no further than James Forman, one of the foremost embezzlers of his time. Perhaps the original white-collar criminal, his appetite for the good life nearly brought down Nova Scotia's largest bank in 1870. Greed drove Maurice Doyle and brothers George and John Boutilier to commit murder; ultimately, the items they stole proved beyond doubt their guilt. As for revenge, Nicholas Martin took the law into his own hands in Sydney in the mid-1850s, gunning down the man he accused of raping his daughter. The result was a morality play that laid bare the uglier side of a repressive Victorian society. And both *Bluenose* skipper Angus Walters and Annabella Hubert, a Cape Breton woman who claimed she was cheated out of her land, turned to the courts seeking justice for wrongs inflicted by others.

But these stories — and the characters that emerge from them — truly run from the sublime to the ridiculous. A.B. MacGillivray's one liners and off-colour jokes may not speak well of judicial office, but his wit has overshadowed his shortcomings on the bench. Digby farmer Isaiah Hill ran up an enormous legal bill simply because he felt his ox was wrongly seized over an $8.50 tax bill. James Maggs, a janitor, took the fall — and claimed the notoriety — for some anonymous newspaper writer who had libelled a public official. And Thomas Chandler Haliburton, creator of the fast-talking American pedlar Sam Slick, was a good judge, a better writer, but one poor businessman.

There's a lot of history within these pages, and insights into the kinds of behaviour our ancestors considered appropriate; but there's as much wit as wisdom. *Bluenose Justice* is an eclectic mix of the slightly offbeat and the deadly serious that I hope you'll find informative as well as entertaining.

* * *

I have been fascinated by Nova Scotia's rich legal heritage for a decade, ever since my first assignment to cover a trial as a rookie reporter. Many of the stories in this collection have appeared over the years in *The Novascotian*, *The Chronicle-Herald* and *The Mail-Star* Friday supplement named after Joseph Howe's famous newspaper. Most have been reworked and expanded for this book. Two stories — the legal ordeal of Nicholas Martin, and James Forman's massive fraud — appear in print for the first time.

I'd like to thank everyone who has helped make this book a reality. Pam Sword gave the manuscript a final and much-needed proofread. Staff of the Public Archives of Nova Scotia in Halifax, the Beaton Institute in Sydney, and the Halifax Herald library fielded numerous requests for information and photographs. But the driving force behind this book was Lesley Choyce of Pottersfield Press, who wanted a follow-up to *Crime Wave* and refused to take no for an answer. His prodding was always gentle, and I appreciate his perseverance.

Dean Jobb
Halifax
June 1993

Part One

LARGER THAN LIFE

Wisecracking A.B. MacGillivray may well have been the wittiest, most irreverent judge ever to grace the bench in Canada (*Chronicle-Herald/Mail-Star* files)

chapter 1

Keep 'em Laughing

It was obvious to everyone watching the daily parade through Glace Bay police court that the eyewitness was being evasive. And that meant everyone, including the presiding magistrate. Asked repeatedly to describe an incident that left two people dead, the witness maintained he had dropped to the ground as soon as the shooting started, and saw nothing.

"I thought I was shot," he protested.

"You mean you ought to be shot," a frustrated A.B. Mac-Gillivray snapped from the bench.

The uncomfortable man on the witness stand was by no means the first person to feel the sting of MacGillivray's sharp tongue. The man who was the law in Glace Bay from the turn of the century to the Second World War — known to everyone as "A.B." — produced a steady stream of one-liners at the expense of witnesses, accused and lawyers alike. Even today, half a century after his death, stories showcasing MacGillivray's caustic wit are swapped in his native Cape Breton and beyond. "He's a legend, the genuine article," noted Peter MacDonald, an Ontario lawyer who has turned a passion for humorous courtroom stories into a literary sideline, most notably the series of *Court Jesters* books. "There are even children in Cape Breton who can rattle off one 'A.B.' story after another."

Like the time MacGillivray was handing down a sentence for a petty crime.

"I'm fining you $25 ..." the magistrate began.

"Why, that's easy," the convicted man piped up. "I've got that in my arse pocket."

"... and thirty days in the county jail," MacGillivray continued, hardly missing a beat. "Have you got that in your arse pocket?"

Then there was the defence lawyer who tried MacGillivray's patience — or, more accurately, lack of patience — with a long-winded legal argument to close out the trial of two men charged with stealing a dozen chickens. Finally, sensing that the judge might have heard enough, the lawyer stopped in mid-sentence.

"Your Honour, I hope I haven't taken up too much of your time."

"Well, I'm not going to stop you," MacGillivray replied, pulling out his pocket watch and taking a look for theatrical effect. "You can talk as long as you want. But I think you'd better know something. The longer you keep me from my dinner, the longer those tramps will roost in the county jail." Ouch.

In another case, a sailor charged with drunkenness came before the Glace Bay court. The accused could speak little English and MacGillivray had a tough time extracting any useful information. Stymied, he inquired about the man's religious beliefs. Did he believe in God? The sailor indicated he didn't believe in anything. "In that case," cracked MacGillivray, unable to resist a straight line, "I'll put you down as a Presbyterian."

* * *

The quick-witted judge who became a legend was born in the village of Grand Narrows, on the Bras d'Or Lakes, in 1858. Alexander Bernard MacGillivray was the eldest of six children whose father was a farmer and justice of the peace. By the time MacGillivray reached his teens the family had moved to Glace Bay, lured by the hope of finding jobs in the coal mines.

At age thirteen MacGillivray began working in the pits, putting in time at several collieries in the area. Then he switched to surface work, loading coal onto ships. In 1882 he married Mary

Johnstone, or "Mary A.B." as she was known to avoid confusion with the legion of other Mary MacGillivrays on the island. They raised seven children.

Along the way MacGillivray's prospects went from good to better. In 1890 he assumed to the post of shipping superintendent for the General Mining Company in Glace Bay. But four years later he abandoned the coal industry for a new career. At thirty-six he was appointed stipendiary (salaried) magistrate for Cape Breton County. When Glace Bay was incorporated in 1901, he became the town's first magistrate. That made him the final judge of those charged with breaching town bylaws and minor offences like drunkenness and shoplifting. He was also required to preside over preliminary hearings for those facing more serious crimes.

Legal training was not a prerequisite for the magistrate's chair in those days, and there is no evidence MacGillivray, to that point at least, had ever cracked a law book. But he looked the part of a judge. He was an imposing figure — more than six feet tall — and managed to strike a scholarly air with an carefully trimmed goatee. Vain about his appearance, he usually wore a wing collar and black bow tie, topping off the package with a derby when he was not in court. But despite his formal attire, his face betrayed the jokester within. MacGillivray, his hair white with age, stares out from a surviving photograph with an impish grin and eyes that seem to brim with mischief. "As he approaches the half-century mark as a magistrate," the *Cape Breton Post* observed in 1933, "A.B. still boasts the upright carriage, deep voice and cheery smile which have been lifelong characteristics."

MacGillivray held court in a small red building on Glace Bay's main street, near the railway tracks. The modest courthouse, which doubled as the judge's office, was little more than "a one-room shack" by one description. It was here that the dapper MacGillivray, the star of the show, dispensed justice and treated onlookers to his memorable punchlines.

He brought a commonsense approach to the bench, which is hardly surprising given his first-hand knowledge of hard work in the mines. "You'd find his ilk in a Lunenburg fisherman or a

Halifax dockworker," says Leo McIntyre, a retired provincial court judge who watched MacGillivray in action in the 1930s. He had only a layman's understanding of the law, but by one account he rarely missed the mark. "In the thousands of cases which have passed through his jurisdiction," a newspaper reporter claimed near the end of MacGillivray's career, "only once has his decision been reversed by a higher court."

Absence of legal training probably explains his abiding distaste for lawyers. "Although he respected the lawyers who appeared before him, he was not particularly fond of them," Louis Dubinsky once said of MacGillivray. Dubinsky, who went on to become a Supreme Court judge, learned that lesson through personal experience. As a rookie lawyer, Dubinsky's first case was the defence of two Glace Bay men charged with stealing chickens; he was the lawyer who earned his clients a longer jail term by keeping MacGillivray from his dinner.

MacGillivray could be as crude as he was blunt. Accustomed to speaking his mind, he sometimes ruffled feathers with the earthy language he used in court. Many of the stories that live on after him are "a little naughty," admits Peter MacDonald, who has collected numerous examples of MacGillivray's wit. "This was a man who said anything that popped into his head." He once dismissed a lawyer's argument as "bullshit." And in his hands, rape cases became a forum for crude remarks and showing off a sexist attitude that would spark outraged editorials and calls for his resignation if uttered from the bench today, and rightly so. MacGillivray was fluent in the Gaelic of his ancestors, prompting one wag to suggest the magistrate was able to speak three languages: "The English language on the bench, Gaelic when with his Scottish friends, and bad language when he's riled."

But MacGillivray, warts and all, is best remembered for his mastery of a fourth language — humour. It's hard to establish if all the A.B. stories are true, and one suspects many have been embellished, or attributed to him over the years as his reputation grew. Dubinsky, who should know, once claimed that many A.B. stories were "figments of the teller's imagination." But one thing is certain, legend or not — MacGillivray was an extremely funny man.

Dubinsky himself swears that one classic line came from MacGillivray's lips. A man charged with possession of stolen goods, the story goes, appeared for trial without a lawyer — certainly no handicap in MacGillivray's court. After the prosecution rested its case, the defendant was adamant that he had no idea the items in question were stolen. MacGillivray then asked the man if he had anything to say to sum up his case. With that, the accused jumped to his feet and shouted: "As God is my judge, I am not guilty."

MacGillivray must have flashed that mischievous grin as he delivered a punchline and verdict rolled into one.

"He's not. I am. And you are."

* * *

Leo McIntyre, an unabashed MacGillivray fan, has lamented that characters like A.B. are few and far between today. Then again, it can be argued that judicial office should be the preserve of those with legal training and a sense of fairness and public service, not stand-up comics. MacGillivray's antics did little for the public image of the province's lowest court. A Nova Scotia politician who was a younger contemporary of MacGillivray, Gordon Rompkey, once remarked that the greatest accomplishment of the magistrates was the production of "tales" that were "good for a laugh."

Wisecracks notwithstanding, there were those who felt the situation in Nova Scotia's magistrate's court was no laughing matter. Besides lacking legal training, stipendiary magistrates were allowed, even expected, to supplement their income through court costs levied on top of the fines they imposed. And that lead to the appearance, if not the reality, of convictions being handed down based on the need to line a magistrate's pockets rather than on the weight of the evidence.

7

As early as 1916, an opposition politician rose in the legislature and charged that "four-fifths of the practising magistrates in Cape Breton were crooked and dishonest." The proof, he charged, was the fact that few had filed mandatory reports with the government disclosing fines and penalties imposed in their courts. *The Halifax Herald,* a newspaper fervently opposed to the Liberal party then in power, used the outburst to condemn the situation in Cape Breton's lower courts as "nothing short of a public scandal." Names were never put to the allegation, but it's likely MacGillivray, a Liberal appointee, was lumped in with the tainted majority.

The government ignored the allegations as grandstanding, and nothing was done. By the early 1930s Mr. Justice W.L. Hall, a Supreme Court judge and a former attorney general, was attacking the fee system as "absolutely vicious." He called for the firing of all sitting magistrates and their replacement with lawyers paid only salary.

The provincial government was finally prodded into action in 1938. A new act created the post of police magistrate, responsible for adjudicating cases previously in the domain of the stipendiary magisrates. The new court officers were forbidden from taking fees, and legal training was finally recognized as an asset; police magistrates were required to have practised law in Nova Scotia for at least three years. Legal scholars hailed the long-overdue changes as "the greatest advance in the administration of law in Nova Scotia" in more than fifty years.

But the idea of starting from scratch was rejected: MacGillivray and other hold-overs from the earlier era were allowed to serve out their time until retirement, or ill-health or death passed their verdicts. MacGillivray, now nearly an octogenarian, was ready to move on anyway. Three years after the magistrate's court was reformed, and forty-seven years after taking his place behind the bench, MacGillivray retired in 1941. He died of a stroke two years later at eighty-four.

A sense of humour will never be a barrier to judicial office, but it's unlikely MacGillivray's legacy of one-liners from the bench will ever be rivalled.

chapter 2

Poison Pen

The letter published in *The Novascotian* on New Year's Day, 1835, was nothing less than an indictment of the actions of some of Halifax's most powerful public officials. Signed with the pseudonym "The People," it alleged that each year £1,000 belonging to "the poor and distressed" was "pocketed by men whose services the country might well spare" — namely the dozen magistrates responsible for governing the city. The letter went on to charge that these magistrates, "by one stratagem or other," had been fleecing the public for the previous three decades, meaning the public purse has been lightened to the tune of roughly £30,000.

The magistrates, furious at having their scruples openly questioned in the press, did not wait long to strike back. Within a week, they pressed Nova Scotia's attorney general to launch a libel prosecution. The object of their wrath was *The Novascotian*'s upstart, thirty-year-old editor and proprietor, Joseph Howe. He hadn't written the scathing letter — it had been submitted by one of his friends, George Thompson — but that made no difference. Howe, as editor, was legally responsible for the contents of his newspaper. He was charged with criminal libel, accused of "wickedly, maliciously and seditiously desiring and intending to stir up and excite discontent among His Majesty's subjects." If convicted, Howe could look forward to a heavy fine or a lengthy term as a guest in one of His Majesty's prisons.

It has been better than a century and a half since Howe stood before a jury and single-handedly mounted his defence to the libel charge. The trial was barely more than a day long, but it

Joseph Howe took on the Halifax establishment in an 1835 courtroom showdown that propelled him into public life. (*Chronicle-Herald/Mail-Star* files)

stands as a landmark in Nova Scotia history. No guided tour of Province House in Halifax is complete without a stop at the ornate legislative library, the scene of Howe's courtroom show-down, where a bronze plaque marks the event. Overnight, the trial made Howe a political force to be reckoned with, signalling the beginning of a political career that would thrust him into the forefront of the battle for responsible government and, later, the fight against Confederation. The trial also spelled the end of the line for several of the more corrupt magistrates whose misdeeds he had laid bare.

Later generations would come to regard Howe's trial as a watershed, establishing the principle of freedom of the press in Canada. But the case did nothing to rewrite the law governing how nineteenth-century journalists did their jobs. From a legal standpoint, the trial is memorable mainly because a jury ignored the letter of the law and returned a verdict in Howe's favour. Howe's real legacy was showing that one person, armed with a belief in the truth and convinced of the rightness of his cause, could do battle with the powers that be — and triumph.

* * *

In the 1830s, local government in Nova Scotia was in the hands of magistrates appointed by the colonial administration. In Halifax, the colony's largest centre, the magistrates directly or indirectly supervised the operation of the police department, poor asylum and other public institutions. Below the magistrates in the evolv-ing bureaucracy were grand jurors — middle-class property owners chosen by lot to keep tabs on the magistrates. By the time Howe became a member of the grand jury in 1832, that body was beginning to flex its muscles, taking the magistrates to task for the sorry state of many government services.

Howe outlined some of the abuses in the course of his trial. The magistrate in charge of the city prison had turned the institu-tion into his private preserve — storing vegetables in the cells, stabling his horse in the woodshed, using inmates to make shoes for his family. The poor asylum — the last refuge for those down on their luck — received inferior, overpriced supplies under the management of its director, another magistrate. By the latter part of 1834, *The Novascotian* had begun a print campaign against the corrupt practices of the magistrates. The war of words culminated in the no-holds-barred letter of January 1, 1835.

After the libel charge was laid, Howe consulted several lawyers. They were unanimously of the opinion that he had no defence. The law of the time was clear: publication of anything that was intended to disturb the public peace or injure the reputations of individuals was libellous and a crime. Well, what if the allegations as published were true? In the eyes of the law, that meant nothing. The sole issue for the jury to decide was whether the libel amounted to a breach of the peace.

But here lay Howe's only hope. If he could prove his allegations, then it followed that he had not published the offending letter with the intention of breaching the peace. Technically speaking, that was still libel — but it was the kind of argument that might sway a jury. Gathering evidence to support the charges against the magistrates turned out to be easy. An appeal for help published by a competing newspaper, *The Acadian Recorder*, did the trick. The next day, Howe recalled, throngs of people crammed his office, "every one of whom had suffered some exaction, had some complaint to expose, or had had justice denied or delayed."

There's an old saw that anyone who represents themselves in court has a fool for a client. But since the law was not on his side, Howe decided he'd rather be foolish than throw in the towel. If he had "the nerve and power to put the whole case before a jury," he reasoned, "and they were fair and reasonable men, they must acquit."

* * *

The trial opened March 2, 1835, in the Supreme Court chamber in Province House — a small room that seems larger thanks to a high ceiling, now home to the legislative library. In those days, balconies lined three of the four walls to accommodate spectators, and the judges' bench squatted in front of high windows that overlooked Halifax's bustling Hollis Street. The quarters were "crammed to overflowing" with onlookers, and "hot as a furnace," according to Howe's description. A number of judges were on the bench for such an important trial, but from them, Howe expected little. His best hope rested with the jurors, and as luck would have it, five of the twelve had served with Howe on the grand jury a few years earlier. They were precisely the kind of men who would be receptive to the sentiments expressed in the letter that had sparked the trial.

The Crown's case was in the hands of Attorney General Samuel Archibald and James F. Gray, a senior lawyer often tapped to assist the prosecution. Gray delivered the opening address, which amounted to a blunt direction to the jury to convict. "It is impossible for the jury to say there is not sufficient defamatory, malicious matter in this letter to constitute libel," he said. Another newspaperman was called to the witness stand to establish that the letter had been published, but that testimony became a formality after Howe acknowledged he had printed it. The letter from "The People" was then read into the court record.

And that was that. The Crown had only to prove that the alleged libel had been published, and the words amounted to libel. With those housekeeping chores out of the way, the prosecutors rested their case and waited for a conviction.

Now it was Howe's turn. He had pored over books on libel law for a week to try to hammer out a defence, and spent another week preparing a speech to the jury. One observer has suggested Howe actually benefited from the lack of professional legal help. Judges have traditionally bent over backwards to appear fair to anyone unable — or unwilling — to retain a lawyer. Howe's biographer, retired Dalhousie University political scientist J. Murray Beck, pointed out that a lawyer would have been limited to arguing the law, which was definitely not on the side of this accused. Howe could "come up with an unorthodox defence and, as a layman, be given wide leeway to use it."

He did just that. For more than six hours Howe marshalled his case, turning the courtroom into a forum to expose fresh examples of abuse among the high and mighty. He cited case after case of corrupt practices by the magistrates, singling out some of the worst offenders by name. Those with ringside seats for the trial made no secret of whose side they were on — Chief Justice Brenton Halliburton was forced to ask spectators to keep their applause to a minimum.

Then Howe took his arguments to a higher plane. He pleaded that Nova Scotia's press should receive "the same rational protection" afforded the press in Britain, where juries were less likely to hand down a libel conviction. "Your verdict will be the most important in its consequences ever delivered before this tribunal," he predicted, challenging the jurors "to leave an unshackled press as a legacy to your children." It was a masterful performance, all the more remarkable because Howe, to that point, had rarely spoken in public. One juryman was reportedly moved to tears.

Howe's exhaustive speech made it impossible to finish the trial that day. Next morning, the attorney general summed up the Crown's case. If ever there was a tough act to follow, this was it, and Archibald made no attempt to match Howe's oratory. He warned the jury that much of what they had heard the previous day was hearsay — second-hand evidence — and no lawyer would have been allowed to go to such lengths. Chief Justice Halliburton, the target of some of Howe's barbs in the past, left no doubt where he stood as he closed the case. "In my opinion the paper charged is a libel, and your duty is to state by your verdict that it is libellous," he solemnly instructed the jurors. But, he added half-heartedly, "you are not bound by my opinion. You are not to be influenced by my feelings, but to pronounce upon the case before you according to the sober convictions of your own minds."

It took the jurors just ten minutes to apply their "sober convictions" and return a verdict of not guilty. Cheers echoed through the Supreme Court chamber and the celebration spilled onto the streets of Halifax. Supporters formed their sleighs into a

A scene from Joseph Howe's libel trial is captured in relief at the foot of his statue in Halifax. (Author photo)

victory parade in Howe's honour. But there was little joy among the city's scandal-tainted magistrates; within days of the verdict, six resigned. The post was so thoroughly discredited that the government had a tough time finding anyone willing to take their place. Howe had solidified his reputation as champion of the common man. His gutsy performance in the courtroom was the springboard for a political career that would one day lead him to the premier's office.

* * *

"It is often stated that Howe established the freedom of the press through his acquittal," Beck wrote of the trial. "This is a myth that has little basis in fact." Howe himself did nothing to discourage the myth-making — in the first edition of *The Novascotian* published in the wake of the trial, he boldly declared that "the press of Nova Scotia is free." Some historians have jumped on the bandwagon and given credence to Howe's inflated view of the trial. W.H. Kesterton, for instance, in his history of Canadian journalism, described Howe's trial as "the most momentous freedom-of-the-press precedent" of the early nineteenth century.

But the case of *The King versus Howe* did nothing to ease the strict laws that governed what newspaper editors could publish without risking a criminal prosecution. A 1980s report of the Law Reform Commission of Canada, which called for the abolition of the outdated offence of criminal libel, outlined the development of Canada libel law without even mentioning Howe's finest hour. "The law is not changed by the verdicts of juries," explained Joseph Chisholm, a Nova Scotia chief justice who was among Howe's greatest admirers. "It is sometimes disregarded by juries in their verdicts." An accommodating jury had saved Howe's bacon, but its verdict did not rewrite the law.

Yet Howe's brilliant defence has left a legacy. The trial showed the folly of using the criminal law to try to stifle dissent in the press. By pressing the charge against Howe, the government gave him a public platform to hammer away at the corrupt practices of the magistrates. And the jury's acquittal served notice that the public was in no mood to tolerate such abuses.

Howe's prosecution was not the last for criminal libel, but it undoubtedly helped speed up the trend toward settling libel claims through the civil courts, punishing libellous press reports with damage awards rather than the spectre of prison. A lawsuit was still an effective check on the printing of unfounded allegations, though. Howe's successor at the helm of *The Novascotian*, Richard Nugent, was bankrupted by damages awarded in a series of libel suits in the early 1840s.

While Howe did not change the libel law, the law was changing. In 1843 the British Parliament passed a law allowing newspaper publishers to claim the truth of a statement as a defence to libel, providing they could show the statement was published for the public good. It would be another three decades before Canadian lawmakers followed suit and enacted similar provisions. Libel is still on the books as a crime in Canada, despite the Law Reform Commission's recommendation that it be abolished. Prosecutions, however, are rare.

chapter 3

Randell's Last Stand

Jack Randell, a tough Newfoundland-born skipper and decorated war veteran, had a taste for adventure. His motto: "Once a scrapper, always a scrapper." It's not surprising, then, that on the morning of March 22, 1929, he found himself in the Gulf of Mexico on a schooner crammed with illegal booze, under heavy fire from a United States Coast Guard cutter. Bullets ripped through the sails and rigging of the rumrunner *I'm Alone*, and water poured into the hull through holes blasted by explosive shells. But as he tried to keep his balance on the deck of his sinking ship, Randell was as stubborn and defiant as ever. "No damn you," he shouted as he jumped into the sea. "You may sink me if you like, but I will not surrender."

Fished out of the water by the Americans, Randell and his crew were put in leg irons and taken to jail in New Orleans. By his own admission, Randell had been trying to smuggle liquor into the U.S., a country that was still bone-dry after a decade of prohibition. In Canada, though, one newspaper hailed Randell as "an international hero for upholding British naval traditions on the high seas." In Ottawa, a member of Parliament condemned the sinking as "an act of deliberate piracy" at best, and "an act of war" at worst.

Canadians had good reason to be outraged. *I'm Alone* had been well outside American waters — and beyond the reach of U.S. law — when it was sent to the bottom. And although the schooner flew the British flag, it had been registered in the port of Lunenburg, Nova Scotia. Randell and *I'm Alone* became the centre of one of the strangest episodes in Canadian diplomatic history.

The rumrunner *I'm Alone*, shown at dockside in Lunenburg, gave the U.S. Coast Guard a run for its money in 1929. (Knickle Studio, Lunenburg)

* * *

There was nothing strange about finding one of the Lunenburg fishing fleet's sleek schooners engaged in the shady business of rumrunning. Once prohibition became law in the U.S. in 1920, there was no shortage of seasoned Canadian sailors and fishermen willing to help quench Uncle Sam's thirst. During the early twenties, the promise of a fast buck lured many Lunenburg vessel owners away from fishing and into the smuggling trade. All a captain had to do was drop anchor just outside American waters at a pre-arranged spot and wait; speedboats from the mainland would show up to ferry the lucrative cargo ashore, taking all the risks. As the decade progressed, however, such small-time operators were squeezed out by larger, more businesslike syndicates controlled by Americans.

One of those rumrunning organizations sent an agent to Nova Scotia in the fall of 1928. The agent, "Big Jamie" Clark, was looking for a good rumrunning vessel — fast, yet capable of carrying a sizeable cargo. Such a boat was up for sale in Lunenburg, the 125-foot, ninety-ton schooner *I'm Alone*. A product of the same shipyard that built the famous racing schooner *Bluenose*, *I'm Alone* sported twin, one hundred-horsepower diesel engines. There was little doubt it could give the fastest coast guard cutter a run for its money. Clark plunked down $18,000 to buy the vessel and began looking for a skipper.

His choice was Jack Randell, a no-nonsense captain who has spent most of his fifty years at sea. Randell had tried his hand at rumrunning on occasion but was between jobs in Liverpool, just down the shore from Lunenburg. When Clark offered him $500 a month to take command of *I'm Alone* and run booze along the Gulf coast, Randell jumped at the chance of spending, as he put it, "a winter in tropical waters at good pay, as against a winter in Nova Scotia in enforced idleness." In November 1928, Randell sailed *I'm Alone* to St. Pierre and Miquelon, picked up 1,500 cases of liquor, and headed south.

The rendezvous with boats from the U.S. was at Trinity Shoals, about twelve miles off the Louisiana shoreline. For the next few months *I'm Alone* made regular runs between that point and Belize, the capital of British Honduras. There were several brushes with the coast guard, but deft seamanship enabled Randell to elude capture. In February 1929 *I'm Alone* was shadowed for two days by the coast guard vessel *Dexter*, commanded by Captain Powell. On the second night Randell finally outwitted Powell and slipped away in the darkness. Word soon reached Belize that *Dexter's* captain was out to get *I'm Alone*.

On the morning of March 20, Randell dropped anchor at a point he estimated to be between fourteen and fifteen miles off the U.S. coast. *I'm Alone* was on its way to yet another rendezvous, laden with just over $62,000 worth of scotch, rye, rum and assorted champagnes and liqueurs. About dawn, spotting the steam-driven coast guard cutter *Wolcott* closing in from the west, Randell made a dash for the open sea. By half-past six, *Wolcott*

19

was close enough to hail *I'm Alone*. When there was no response, *Wolcott*'s captain fired three blank rounds and again issued an order to stop. "I'll see you in hell first," Randell bellowed back through a megaphone. "I'm on the high seas and you have no jurisdiction over me."

After a three-hour chase, Randell finally agreed to let Frank Paul, *Wolcott*'s commander, come on board to continue the jurisdictional debate at closer quarters. Unarmed, Paul rowed over to *I'm Alone* as his crew kept the deck gun, now loaded with a live round, trained on the schooner. To Randell's surprise, Paul was still wearing his slippers.

The two men went below to discuss the standoff. Randell contended the coast guard had no jurisdiction over his vessel; Paul argued just as strenuously that he did. It all depended on *I'm Alone*'s position when sighted by *Wolcott*. That was "a matter of navigation," Randell insisted, "and if I am nothing else in the world, I am a navigator." Randell reckoned he had been at least fourteen miles offshore. But Paul said the schooner was less than eleven miles from the coast. Under a doctrine known as hot pursuit, he had the right to stop and search a suspected rumrunner sighted within the U.S. twelve-mile limit, no matter how far the chase extended into international waters. After making no progress through diplomacy, Paul returned to his vessel.

The two boats maintained a southerly course into the Gulf of Mexico. Then, about two in the afternoon, Paul decided to take more decisive measures. *Wolcott* steamed up to the schooner flying signal flags demanding: "Heave to or I fire." Randell ignored the ultimatum, and *Wolcott* began firing shells into *I'm Alone*'s sails and rigging. When the cutter's deck gun jammed after about twenty rounds, the crew opened fire with rifles and machine guns. "Suddenly, I felt a sharp blow in the front of my right thigh," recalled Randell, who was standing near the schooner's stern. "The whole leg went numb. I staggered, but I caught my balance. I looked down expecting to see the blood running." Luckily for Randell, he had been struck by a dummy bullet made of wax.

Wolcott ceased firing and dropped astern, but refused to give up the chase. At dusk, when *I'm Alone*'s crew hauled down the Union Jack, they discovered it had been pierced by a shell. For a man who had fought under that flag in battle, it was the last straw. "If I had had a three-pounder [gun] on board, that cutter would have gone down quick," he later vowed. Randell defiantly signalled *Wolcott*: "Captain, you have made a grave error. You have mutilated my flag."

The pursuit continued for two days. By March 22, *I'm Alone* was well over two hundred miles off the U.S. coast. With its deck gun jammed and useless, *Wolcott* had radioed for help. At half-past seven that morning, *Dexter* joined the chase. *Dexter*'s captain, Powell, had been outwitted by Randell once; he was determined it would not happen again. Powell issued a final order to stop, then opened fire.

Let Randell describe the scene that followed: "The *Dexter* went into action like a miniature battleship ... four pounder explosive shells, machine gun bullets, rifle bullets, came whistling at us point blank at a range of less than 200 yards." Randell and his crew could only gather at the stern as *I'm Alone* was literally shot out from under them. As water began to rush into the hold, Randell ordered his men to abandon ship. One, a Frenchman named Leon Mainguy, drowned before he could be picked up by the coast guard cutters.

From his cell in New Orleans, Randell called the sinking "the most cowardly attack on a merchant ship since the submarine warfare" of the 1914-1918 war. Randell and his crew were charged with conspiracy to violate the prohibition laws, but the Americans eventually dropped the case in the face of public pressure. The Canadian government vehemently protested the sinking as a breach of international law and took the matter to arbitration. In 1935, the U.S. government formally apologized for sending the schooner to the bottom and paid $25,000 in restitution to the crew.

As for Randell, he enjoyed the notoriety and within a year cranked out an autobiography entitled, fittingly, *I'm Alone*. But his free-wheeling days on the high seas were over. The proud skipper who had sparked an international incident ended his seafaring days as master of a small steamer plying the calmer waters of the Great Lakes.

Part Two

HIGH-CLASS CROOKS

Prolific embezzler James Forman had trouble telling the difference between the Bank of Nova Scotia's books and his own pocketbook. (*Chronicle-Herald/Mail-Star* files)

chapter 4

Cooking the Books

I t could have been called the Bank of Forman. James Forman had been running the Bank of Nova Scotia for close to four decades — since the institution was founded in 1832, to be precise. As cashier, he was in charge of operations at the bank's main office, only a stone's throw away from the bustling wharves that were the lifeblood of Halifax's economy. Forman took it upon himself to do the bookkeeping, using quill and leather-bound ledgers to keep track of money held on deposit, loaned to local businessmen, or tied up in the gold and silver specie that backed the bank's paper money. The Bank of Nova Scotia was one of the largest financial institutions in the Maritimes; by 1870 slightly more than $2.1 million in assets — a staggering sum at the time — was under Forman's direct control.

Forman, who turned seventy-five that year, could have in-spired the term "hands-on manager." Stooped with age, with a salt-and-pepper beard, baggy eyes, and his remaining hair com-bed only by the wind, Forman could have been mistaken for an elderly customer who had wandered behind the wickets. But his face bore an expression as mean as a bulldog's, and few ques-tioned his orders. Forman, you see, was not just another employee. While he was only a notch above the lowly clerks in the bank's hierarchy, he vastly outstripped them in social stand-ing. Like the merchants and lawyers who served on the bank's board of directors, he lived in a posh estate amidst the quiet, tree-lined streets of the city's south end.

Besides being the Bank of Nova Scotia's most powerful and longest-serving employee, Forman was its most trusted. He had his own set of keys to the vault, affording him round-the-clock access to the bank's cash; that was a privilege enjoyed by only one other official, the president. And rather than being saddled with the mundane task of tabulating figures at the office, Forman was free to pack up the bank's books and work on them at home in the evenings. No one dared question such unusual practices, not even the directors who took turns working weekly stints at the bank. Forman had the complete confidence of the man at the bank's helm, his close friend Mather Byles Almon. President since 1837, Almon was a wealthy Halifax merchant and one of the bank's founders. He was also agent for the giant General Mining Association, which had exclusive rights to mine Nova Scotia coal — a lucrative account Almon had brought into the bank's fold. Over the years he had come to rely heavily on Forman, who was two years his senior and had been with the bank as long as anyone could remember. By 1870, with Almon's health failing and his eyesight nearly gone, the reliance upon Forman's judgment and integrity was complete.

So it was an act of immense bravery when a junior clerk by the name of Johns approached the bank's accountant, J.C. Mackintosh, one day in the spring of 1870 to point out something in the books that just didn't add up. By his reckoning, a large sum — about $30,000 — was unaccounted for. Johns had "looked upon it as an error for over a month," and said nothing. But after another month of trying to reconcile the figures, the clerk later noted, "there was enough to satisfy me there was a false entry."

The revelation confirmed suspicions Mackintosh had been harbouring about his boss. As accountant, he knew Forman's personal account at the bank had been overdrawn for some time. For the past couple of years, he had been carrying out a clandestine audit of the figures Forman had recorded at the end of each banking day. But since Forman alone made the entries, Mackintosh had little luck determining if the figures matched the money flowing through the bank's coffers.

Now, it appeared, Forman had become sloppy in his old age. After taking a couple of months to recheck his math and summon his courage, Mackintosh went to Almon in July 1870 to report serious discrepancies in the books kept by the president's good friend, James Forman. But $30,000 was only the tip of the iceberg — Forman had been systematically looting the Bank of Nova Scotia's vault for at least twenty-five years, helping himself to more than ten times that amount. A junior clerk's sharp eye proved to be the beginning of the end for one of the most successful embezzlers of all time.

* * *

By 1870 the Bank of Nova Scotia had established itself as a pillar of the province's financial community — the place where successful businessmen like shipping magnate Samuel Cunard kept their accounts. But when it had come into being a generation earlier, in the 1830s, it had been an upstart institution, the nemesis of Halifax's business and political elite. In fact, it was created for the sole purpose of challenging that clique's stranglehold on local commerce.

By the early 1800s, Nova Scotia's economy — based on farming, fishing, shipbuilding and overseas trade — was mature enough to support a bank. Merchants required a source of credit, and there was a desperate need some form of currency that was acceptable to all. Gold and silver coins, be they Spanish doubloons or British sovereigns, were considered the best form of legal tender, but few merchants wanted to cart around tubs of coins as they went about their business.

The solution was a bank that could loan money and put its own notes in circulation, backed by gold and silver held in its vaults. Between 1801 and 1825, four bills were put before the Nova Scotia assembly to incorporate a bank; each was defeated because of a clause making the proposed bank a monopoly. Politicians in rural areas of the province balked at putting all that commercial power in the hands of a single institution based in the capital, Halifax.

What Halifax's business leaders were denied by legislation, however, they managed to create by agreement. In 1825, shortly after the fourth incorporation attempt fizzled in the assembly, eight wealthy Haligonians banded together to form the Halifax Banking Company. The leading lights included Enos Collins, a merchant and shipper reputed to be the richest man in British North America. The new bank set up shop in a corner of a Collins-owned stone warehouse on the waterfront, and became known on the street simply as Collins' Bank. (The word "bank" can still be seen inscribed above the doorway of its former premises, now part of a restoration project called Historic Properties). The only difference between the private bank and the institutions proposed earlier was the lack of a public charter. The monopoly over banking, so long thwarted by the assembly, was now a fact.

Resentment over the Halifax Banking Company's unchecked power soon renewed calls for the creation of a public bank. It was as much a reflection of the rise of a new political order as of rival businessmen seeking a piece of the action. True, many were incensed with the private bank's policies, like redeeming the bulk of its notes in government-issued paper money instead of prized gold and silver. But the prominent figures lobbying for a public bank were also the driving force behind the movement to replace the old order or appointment and privilege with a responsible government, accountable to the elected assembly. Front and centre was J.B. Uniacke, a leading member of the assembly, while Joseph Howe, the man whose name is synonymous with the long struggle for responsible government, cheered on the effort in the pages of his fiesty newspaper, *The Novascotian.*

After scores of potential investors signed on, a bill to incorporate the Bank of Nova Scotia went before the assembly in 1832. There was no talk of monopoly this time around, except to point out that the new bank would eliminate the existing one. After a stormy passage, the bill cleared the assembly by a healthy margin and was forwarded to the council — the appointed upper house — for approval. The chances of winning the council's consent seemed bleak: five of that body's twelve members were partners in the Halifax Banking Company. One of the new bank's backers ventured the opinion that the man in the moon was more likely than the council to approve the bill.

To no one's surprise, the bill came back amended to death. Onerous restrictions tacked on by the council threatened to stop the Bank of Nova Scotia in its tracks. But the howls of outrage in the assembly and the Halifax press eventually convinced the council to temper the worst of its amendments. The bank, saddled with only a handful of new rules governing capital level and increasing the liability of directors, was incorporated on March 30, 1832.

The first board of directors went about starting a bank from scratch with only one minor handicap — no one had hands-on banking experience. Banknotes were ordered from American printers and a newspaper advertisement was placed seeking a suitable building in the centre of town. But the most important step was hiring the new bank's key employee, the cashier. A committee of directors chose James Forman, a thirty-seven-year-old businessman whose credentials were backed by his family's good standing in Halifax society. Forman's father, James, had been partner in a profitable Halifax wholesaling house that specialized in wine, and was among the backers of the first failed attempt to establish a bank in 1801. The son joined the family business right out of school, and took over his father's role in the partnership after 1820. Active in the community, the younger Forman was a leading member of groups as diverse as the Horticultural Association and the Nova Scotia Literary and Scientific Society.

When the idea of setting up a public bank made the rounds in the early 1830s, the younger Forman expressed some interest. He was among those who signed a petition supporting the formation of the Bank of Nova Scotia, but he declined to buy stock in the scheme. The cashier's post, though, was another matter. The directors, for their part, were no doubt pleased to place their bank in the hands of someone who shared their place in society. Add the candidate's friendship with Almon, a leading shareholder who was soon to become president, and Forman's hiring was a foregone conclusion.

The new cashier, granted an annual salary of £300 — more than double that of the two clerks in his charge — was sent to Saint John, New Brunswick, for a crash course in banking. He carried a letter of introduction to the Bank of New Brunswick asking that he be allowed to spend "a few days" observing "the mode of conducting business." That, apparently, was the extent of Forman's formal training. In August 1832, the Bank of Nova Scotia opened its doors for the first time.

The new bank grew rapidly in its early years, adding agencies — the forerunner of branches — in five smaller Nova Scotia communities by 1839. But the initial spurt was followed by decades of slow growth. Dividends paid to shareholders became smaller, and by 1870 the number of agencies had been pared back to three. A series of economic downturns and competition from new banks that sprang up in Halifax in the 1860s partly explained the problem. It was only when serious errors were detected in the books that it became apparent there might be a more insidious reason for the Bank of Nova Scotia's poor performance.

* * *

It fell to Almon to break the bad news to the bank's nine-member board of directors at a hastily convened meeting on July 28, 1870. According to the minutes, "the president informed them that the Cashier, Mr. James Forman, had been guilty of making many fraudulent entries in the books of the Bank, by which he had abstracted a large amount of its funds." Forman had been relieved of his duties and stripped of his keys and account books the night before. Since the cashier's figures could not be trusted, several directors immediately began counting the gold, silver and banknotes in the vault to find out how much money the bank really had on hand.

The next step was facing the shareholders. A brief notice was inserted in Halifax newspapers calling shareholders to a special meeting during the second week of August. No reason was given for the gathering, but word was leaking out that something was seriously wrong. As early as August 2 the bank's agent in Pictou was told to assure customers that their deposits were safe. By the time the shareholders' meeting convened on August 9, rumours had already made their way into the papers that there was a serious shortfall at the bank, and Forman was responsible.

The crowd that showed up was so large that the meeting had to be moved from the bank's boardroom to a nearby government building. Although reporters were locked out, there was no shortage of disgruntled shareholders willing to spill the beans. The directors produced a balance sheet showing Forman had helped himself to an astounding $320,000 over the previous twenty-five years. The cashier had already signed over virtually all his property and belongings — houses, building lots, carriages, the family home, even his silverware — to cover part of the loss. Added to the money put up by Forman's bondholders, an estimated $195,000 could be recovered. That still left the bank roughly $125,000 in the hole.

The directors put on a brave face, insisting that the bank was solvent and would have no problem weathering the crisis. But to maintain the confidence of investors and the public alike, a joint committee of shareholders and directors was struck to thoroughly review the bank's books.

There was still the matter of what to do about Forman. One shareholder called for his arrest, which seemed the natural course. But Forman's doctor, who was on hand for the meeting because he held shares in the bank, protested that the cashier was "now so seriously ill that his life might be endangered by such a course." After a brief discussion, the decision on whether to pursue criminal charges was left to the committee set up to sift through the books.

Not surprisingly, the bank's directors took their share of knocks in the press. How could Forman's massive theft have gone unchecked for so long, editorial writers asked. *The British Colonist*, decidedly Tory in outlook, toed the establishment line, suggesting the directors had been chastened by the experience, and their "negligence or over confidence" would not be repeated. But *The Morning Chronicle* was having none of that.

"Mr. Forman's operations were not so cunningly conducted that they could not be easily discovered," a pointed editorial in the paper's August 16 edition observed. "It was well known that he was engaged in heavy speculations, and that his expenditures were far too great for one of his means. Yet the suspicions of those drowsy Directors were not aroused." The president and directors had allowed more than $300,000 "to slip through their fingers, and it is high time they should either resign their positions or be ejected from them."

As for Forman, *The Chronicle* was inclined to think he should face the full weight of the law — social standing, advanced age and ill-health notwithstanding. "His was not the paltry embezzlement of a few dollars, which has before now sent some needy clerk to the penitentiary, but a gigantic theft," the paper pointed out. "The anguish he must suffer is in itself a heavy punishment. Yet while we imprison the urchin who steals an apple we should not pardon the well-informed, able man who steals hundreds of thousands of dollars." *The Chronicle* passed the buck, saying it was up to the government and the bank's shareholders to decide whether Forman should be prosecuted. "If they are willing that such a gross swindle should go unpunished by the law, perhaps the rest of the community will be satisfied. Perhaps they will not." One church newspaper took a stronger stance, warning that letting Forman off the hook could prove "a temptation" to others to commit crime. "Justice may, in this instance perhaps, be too much tempered with mercy."

But even as the debate raged over whether to call in the police, Forman was making himself scarce. For a man who was too sick to be arrested, he was certainly well enough to travel. One report said he left Halifax in mid-August on the pretext of visiting relatives in northern Nova Scotia; a few days later he turned up in New York. He eventually moved to London to escape the furor.

The bank sold off Forman's former properties at auction in September, including Thorndean, his elegant Halifax mansion that still stands in south-end Halifax. That same month Almon stepped down as president, claiming poor eyesight made it

James Forman's elegant Halifax estate, Thorndean, was signed over to the bank in 1870 after his fraud was exposed. (Author photo)

impossible for him to sign thousands of new banknotes due to be issued. Few doubted his close association with Forman made it impossible for him to stay in office.

Meanwhile, the committee set up to review the books was having little success deciphering Forman's handiwork. An independent auditor — W.C. Menzies of the rival Bank of British North America — was hired to establish how much money Forman had skimmed. At the annual shareholders meeting in March 1871, Menzies gave a final figure down to the last penny — $314,967.68. That was slightly below the initial estimate, but still represented about 15 per cent of the bank's total assets. The sale of Forman's property, on the other hand, was netting less money than hoped. And to make matters worse, the former cashier's bondsmen were disputing how much they should cough up in the wake of the theft. Covering the shortfall ate up an $80,000 reserve fund, all earnings for the first six months of 1870, and close to $28,000 of the bank's capital. Despite the heavy financial burden, a small dividend was paid to mollify the shareholders.

Throughout the embarrassing episode the Bank of Nova Scotia had managed to keep a lid on details of Forman's methods — and the directors' inability to stop him. But all that changed in the spring of 1872, when the battle with Forman's bondsmen spilled into the courts. Five prominent Halifax businessmen had agreed in 1865 to post a bond on Forman's behalf, but only one — Alexander Keith, a Halifax brewer and one of the bank's directors — paid up. The bank elected to sue for the remaining $22,000, and the whole mess was laid bare in a Halifax courtroom.

Menzies, who was taken on as the new cashier after completing the audit, and the clerk who first twigged to the theft took the witness stand to revive the Forman scandal. The new president and three rather sheepish directors also testified. And a letter Forman had written to the bank in late 1870, in which he acknowledged "deficiencies" exceeding $310,000, was read into the record. But the key witness was J.C. Mackintosh, who had been promoted from accountant to deputy cashier after his leading role in uncovering Forman's activities.

Mackintosh revealed that in some cases Forman had swiped tens of thousands of dollars in a single month, including $20,000 stolen soon after he had been bonded. The thefts had begun in 1844, and from the 1850s-on Forman's personal account was overdrawn by as much as $47,000. As for the directors, Mackintosh admitted they were oblivious to the overdraft; as accountant, he was required to report overdrawn accounts to only one official, the cashier. That was just one of many examples of the bank's reliance on Forman's honesty rather than a proper system of internal checks and balances. "The cashier could make alterations [in the books]," Mackintosh admitted, "as many as he liked."

The jury awarded only $12,000 of the $22,000 sought, a move some interpreted as acknowledging that the directors had been asleep at the switch. Undaunted, the bank went back for more punishment, appealing the verdict to the Supreme Court's full bench. The award was upheld, but not before Chief Justice William Young tore a strip off the bank's directors for their "blind confidence" in Forman. "Everything was fair on the surface, and everything rotten below," the judge remarked. "The falsifications on the books were endless." In the wake of this "catastrophe," he was happy to report, the province's banks had taken steps to curb the "tremendous and irresponsible power" their cashiers had enjoyed in the past.

* * *

The Bank of Nova Scotia, for its part, soon rebounded from the Forman affair. With a new cashier and a series of younger, more aggressive presidents, the bank launched a drive to open new agencies and expand business. At the annual shareholders meeting in March 1872, exactly two years after Forman's embezzlement first came to light, the directors proudly declared "that both as respects its finances and credit [the bank] may now be said to have recovered from the effects of the loss by its late Cashier."

Forman was never prosecuted, despite the editorials decrying one form of justice for the rich and another for the poor. There was certainly enough evidence. The bank's decision not to press charges defies an easy explanation, especially when it was willing to wash its dirty linen in public for the sake of trying to squeeze a few thousand dollars from the bondsmen. Forman's ill-health and age were undoubtedly taken into account, since it would have been necessary to extradite him from England to face trial. But the deciding factor may have been the directors' reluctance to further punish one of their own. After all, Forman had rubbed shoulders with the cream of Halifax society, even if it turned out that all the while he was betraying those around him.

Prosecution soon became a moot point. Forman, stripped of his ill-gotten trappings of wealth at age seventy-six, did not have to endure the stigma of his fall from grace for long. James Forman — community leader, trusted employee and prolific embezzler — died in England in August 1871.

chapter 5

An Affair of Honour

Business was slow that Friday morning at Burchell's general store in Sydney. With Christmas barely over, the few people dropping in were more interested in the warmth of the woodstove than the goods on the shelves. Some of the regulars had already put in an appearance, complaining about the winter weather and filling the store with the sharp smell of pipe smoke. But this was no ordinary day; the town was rife with scandalous rumours about a prominent young lawyer and the daughter of a respected public official. George Burchell had heard the whispers, and he knew there was a tragic truth behind them. But he never suspected that the whole mess was about to come to a head right before his eyes.

When Nicholas Martin came through the door, Burchell was glad to see his old friend in a good mood. He looked "calm and collected," Burchell thought — surprising, considering the strain he had been under these past few days. Sydney was a small town, and Martin, former postmaster, justice of the peace and gentleman farmer, was known to everyone. That was one of the reasons there was so much talk on the street. Martin and Burchell talked for a while about nothing in particular while a customer checked out the merchandise. But as soon as they were alone in the store, Martin revealed his real reason for stopping by.

Martin, a tall man of sixty whose brown hair was only now beginning to show a touch of grey, walked over to a open wooden keg filled with nails. He picked up one and asked the price. Four pence a pound, Burchell replied. Martin said he had bought two kegs of nails and some other hardware in order to do some building at his house about a mile from town. But he had "given up the notion," and now he needed money so he could leave Sydney with his daughter, Catherine.

Martin was about to ask Burchell if he would take the building materials off his hands when he was interrupted by the rattle of the front door. It was Reverend Alexander DesBrisay, a Wesleyan minister. The three men exchanged greetings and the conversation turned to the weather. A couple of minutes later Charles McAlpine, a merchant in town from Louisbourg and another mutual acquaintance, entered the store. Martin politely inquired about the health of McAlpine's brother, but he had more pressing matters on his mind. He took Burchell aside and asked if they could speak privately. Burchell lead Martin into the back part of the store, and closed the door.

Martin resumed his plea for cash. Burchell wanted to know how much he hoped to get for the nails and other building supplies, and balked when Martin said £70. Even if he wanted to buy them, Burchell explained, he did not have that kind of money on hand. Martin's face betrayed his disappointment. "It's the only means I have of getting away," he said. "If I could sell the goods, I think I could get off on Captain Lewis' vessel," which was about to sail for the United States.

Burchell understood his friend's plight, but he had more bad news. He had just spoken with another mariner who said the Lewis ship did not have a cabin and was unlikely to take on passengers. Burchell suggested the name of another merchant who might be interested in buying the goods, but Martin's options were growing fewer by the minute. He was trapped, unable to shield his daughter from the vicious gossip or take her away in a desperate bid to erase his family's shame.

With that, Martin opened the door of the back room to leave. Burchell followed, but was shocked to see that someone had come into the store in their absence. There, standing at the stove with his back to them, was none other than Archibald O. Dodd, Esq., a Sydney lawyer and, from Martin's point of view, the source of all the trouble. The timing could not have been worse, and Burchell feared a showdown was in the works. But Martin continued to walk straight toward the door to the street, his hands in the pockets of his overcoat, as if oblivious to Dodd's presence.

Burchell walked a step behind and watched Martin's every move, alert for any sign that he intended to attack Dodd. "If I had seen Martin walk with a quick step, I would have seized him," Burchell claimed. But Martin continued toward the door at a normal pace. Dodd stepped away from the stove and, with his back still to Martin, headed toward the same exit. It's possible he never saw Martin, who was only couple of steps behind him.

It was all over in seconds. In one swift motion, Martin pulled a pistol from his right pocket, stepped forward, pressed the barrel against the back of Dodd's left shoulder and fired. An ear-splitting crack echoed through the store as Dodd, doubled over with pain, staggered toward the counter. Burchell saw a flash of sunlight reflect off the pistol as it was drawn, but he was unable to grab Martin in time. McAlpine and DesBrisay, who were still in the store, could only look on in horror.

Burchell was the first to react. "How dare you do such a thing in my shop?" he screamed. "Go out. Go out." But Martin stood at the door with the smoking pistol in his hand, staring down on Dodd with what Burchell described as "a fiendish look" on his face. Burchell then grabbed Martin by the collar and pushed him out the door backwards. "Now let the public take me," Martin declared as Burchell slammed the door in his face.

Burchell immediately turned his attention to Dodd, who was lying on his side behind the counter. He sent McAlpine and DesBrisay for a doctor, then eased Dodd onto his back and put a bundle of wrapping paper under his head as a makeshift pillow. Dodd was fading fast. "It's no use," Burchell said as Dr. Lewis Johnston and McAlpine rushed into the store minutes later. "He is gone."

But as the doctor searched for a pulse, Dodd drew a breath. McAlpine took off again, this time to fetch Judge Dodd and bring him to his son's side. Johnston opened Dodd's coat and discovered the butt of a pistol that had been tucked inside. It was loaded, and Burchell gingerly placed the gun on a nearby shelf.

Supreme Court judge Edmund Dodd did everything in his power to see that his son's killer was brought to justice. (PANS /Photograph Collection)

The doctor unbuttoned Dodd's vest and shirt, revealing that the bullet had exited through the chest. But there was nothing he could do. Dodd was already dead.

At almost the same moment, his killer walked into the nearby office of a justice of the peace, Peter Clarke. "I have come to surrender myself to you," Martin, his face still flushed with excitement, announced as he took off his scarf. "I have had my revenge. I am a murderer. I have shot Dodd."

"Did you shoot him dead?" was the best response Clarke could muster to the startling admission.

"I saw him fall," Martin replied, as if Clarke was belittling his prowess as an executioner. He dropped to his knees in front of Clarke's desk and began to pray: "God have mercy on me for the act that I have done."

Just then Edward Archbold, a local merchant and one of Martin's closest friends, happened to walk in. Without a word of explanation, Clarke grabbed his coat, asked his latest visitor to keep an eye on Martin, and headed to Burchell's store to see for himself.

There were a few moments of uneasy silence, but Archbold sensed something terrible had happened. He was well aware of the bad blood between the Dodds and the Martins, and the reason Martin wanted so desperately to get out of town. Martin had been at Archbold's store earlier that morning, mean-mouthing the Dodds and trying to pawn off his building materials to raise money. Archbold had agreed to deliver a letter from Martin asking for passage on Captain Lewis's ship and that seemed to do the trick. By the time Archbold had left Martin at the front door of Burchell's store, he had calmed down.

Now, less than an hour later in Clarke's office, Martin brought Archbold up to date. "I have had my revenge," he explained.

"What do you mean?" Archbold asked.

"I have shot Dodd," he stated matter-of-factly, reaching into his pocket and pulling out the pistol to make sure Archbold believed him.

"My God!" Archbold exclaimed. "Which Dodd?"

"Archie."

"When? Where?"

"At Burchell's."

"Are you sure he is dead?"

"I fear he is," replied Martin, who was suddenly sounding less than proud of his accomplishment. He asked Archbold to go and see if Dodd were still alive, but Archbold stood in the doorway and maintained his post as Martin's unofficial guard. "You will know soon enough," he said.

Martin showed little concern about facing a murder charge, asking Archbold if he thought he could earn God's forgiveness by devoting the rest of his life to repentance and prayer. Within minutes, deputy sheriff Richard Logue — summoned once Clarke had confirmed that Dodd was dead — arrived at the office. Martin stepped forward to offer himself for arrest. "I know what you have come for," he told Logue. "Put your hand on my shoulder. I am your prisoner."

Word of the execution-style shooting at the height of the holiday season left Sydney's residents aghast. "This town was the scene yesterday morning of one of the most appalling Tragedies that it has ever fallen to our lot to record, and which deeply convulsed and agitated the whole community," the Sydney-based *Cape Breton News* declared in its New Year's Eve, 1853 edition. Details were sketchy, the paper reported, but the "shocking act" was apparently sparked by "an alleged injury done by [the] deceased to a member of the family of the accused." A coroner's jury had returned a verdict of wilful murder the day of the killing, and Martin was in jail awaiting trial.

The newspaper's editor, James Ward, recognized that the slaying was a double tragedy. "We most sincerely grieve for and commiserate [with] the families of both parties," he wrote. Two of Sydney's most prominent and powerful families — the people who were supposed to be setting an example for the masses — had resorted to cold-blooded murder to resolve their differences. But Martin's act of revenge was more than a case of unusually bad manners — it laid bare the strict moral code of an unforgiving society. In an era when a woman's pregnancy out of wedlock was considered a heinous crime in itself, a distraught father could be capable of anything. The untimely death of Archibald Dodd and the legal ordeal of Nicholas Martin present disturbing insights into the repressive attitudes that pervaded Nova Scotia society in the Victorian era.

* * *

In the 1850s Sydney was a small port town with big aspirations. Its large harbour sheltered a steady stream of ships — square-riggers flying foreign flags and a fleet of locally built vessels — that carried timber and produce from the surrounding countryside to world markets. The strategic importance of the harbour, located on Cape Breton's northern coast, had prompted the British to establish a garrison, further boosting the local economy. But Sydney's role as a trading centre would soon be

Sydney, depicted in this 1850s landscape, was the scene of Nicholas
Martin's cold-blooded murder of a young lawyer he accused of raping
his daughter. (Beaton Institute, University College of Cape Breton)

eclipsed. Nearby mines were beginning to produce large quan-
tities of coal, the black gold that was destined to catapult Sydney
into the industrial age as the site of a sprawling steelmaking
complex.

In the meantime, Sydney boasted no more than a thousand
people and played second fiddle to Arichat, a large fishing centre
on the island's south coast. The town was laid out in a grid of
streets at the tip on a peninsula jutting into a harbour, but it still
had a rural feel. Away from the main street houses were
separated by large fields that supplied the owners' livestock with
hay. "Sydney in the early days ... could justly lay claim to the
possession of pretty homes and many beautiful gardens," one
long-time resident claimed.

It would not be an exaggeration to describe Nicholas Henry
Martin as one of the town's most popular citizens. Barely able to
provide for his own family of eight, he was known for his
generosity to others. "I never saw him turn his back on a poor

man," declared a friend who, as a small boy, had been taken into the Martin household after his own father's death. An educated man given to quoting Shakespeare, Martin was also a staunch supporter of the temperance movement who sometimes lectured on the evils of drink. Unselfishness toward others, coupled with his normally quiet, sunny disposition, made people inclined to overlook Martin's less attractive features — bouts of severe depression and a quick temper.

Born in 1794 just outside Cork, on Ireland's south coast, Martin lived for a time on Prince Edward Island and ended up in Nova Scotia by chance rather than by design. He was on his way back to Britain when his ship went down off Cape Breton. Saved from the wreck, Martin ended up in Arichat, where he met a woman named Kavanagh who soon became his wife. About this time Martin inherited a tidy sum from his mother's estate, and he used the proceeds to go into partnership with an Arichat merchant. But the foray into business went sour, driving him to the brink of bankruptcy. About 1840 Martin moved his six children to a farm near Sydney — christened with the exalted name Sun Lodge. Income from jobs as postmaster and justice of the peace — appointments that speak of good political connections — made him comfortable, but far from wealthy. By 1853 he had handed over the postmaster's job to his oldest son, Robert, and turned his attention full-time to farming.

At age sixty, he finally felt financially secure. He had even managed to put aside enough money to buy some building materials to spruce up his home. But he was not thinking only of himself — his children were grown, but all were still living at home. Martin doted on his children, and none more than Catherine, the younger of his two daughters. Even Kate's siblings agreed that she was his favourite. Martin descibed her to friends in glowing terms: "an amiable girl," he would say, "a more affectionate girl never breathed." One woman, a new acquaintance, claimed he spoke so often of Catherine that it was some time before she realized he even had another daughter. "I never saw so much devotion toward a child by a parent," she said. But there was a downside to all this parental love — it made Martin strict and overprotective. Even though his children were getting older, he expected them to stay around the house. And like most young women of her time, Catherine was forbidden to leave home at night without the "protection" of a chaperone.

The Dodds, unlike the Martins, did not need to earn respect — they commanded it with wealth and high office. Edmund Murray Dodd — war hero, lawyer, politician and now judge — was the scion of one of Cape Breton's most powerful families. His father, Archibald, had served as chief justice of Cape Breton when the island was still a separate colony. Born in 1797, Edmund Dodd joined the Royal Navy as a teenager. Although he was only fifteen when war broke out with the Americans in 1812, Dodd saw action as a midshipman and spent some time as a prisoner of war. He later decided to follow his father's footsteps, gaining admittance to the Nova Scotia bar in 1821.

For Dodd, the law was a stepping stone to a political career. His first political cause was Cape Breton separatism. Sydney, which had enjoyed the perks of being the seat of colonial government, was hit hard by annexation to the mainland in 1820. That year Dodd ran for a seat in the Nova Scotia legislature on a separatist platform, but lost. Not all Cape Bretoners opposed annexation, but most agreed the island was underrepresented in the legislature at Halifax. The result was a compromise — the island remained part of Nova Scotia, but three additional Cape Breton MLAs were added in 1832. Dodd won a by-election to fill the newly created seat for Sydney Township.

Even though he continued to press for a separate Cape Breton, Dodd emerged as an ally of the Tories who were trying to keep their stranglehold on power. He was appointed to the governing executive council in 1838 and became solicitor general in 1844. Having lost the fight against responsible government, he bailed out of politics in 1848 to take an appointment to the Supreme Court. Overshadowed by the great Joseph Howe and other reformers in the legislature, Dodd also was far from a stellar performer on the bench. "Despite his acknowledged ability as a lawyer, he was not a particularly successful judge," noted one biographer. "Increasing deafness combined with a tendency toward tedious and verbose explanation handicapped him."

But when court schedules brought him back to Sydney — where he maintained a spacious estate in the centre of town at an intersection nicknamed Judge's Corner — he still commanded at least the begrudging respect of his neighbours. He conducted himself with the haughty bearing of a man accustomed to acting, and being treated, like a gentleman. The story is told of a time he went bird hunting with a high-ranking officer from a French warship that was visiting Sydney. The Frenchman was about to shoot a snipe as it ran along the ground when Dodd intervened. He was mortified at such a display of bad sportsmanship — shooting a helpless bird before it could take flight. "I'll never go shooting with a man of your stripe again," he said as he called his dog and headed home in disgust.

Archibald, Dodd's oldest son, was named after his illustrious grandfather. Not much is known about Archie Dodd, who had little time to make a name for himself before his fatal run-in with Martin. He had been practising law in Sydney for less than three years when he was gunned down at twenty-seven. But his family's wealth and prestige no doubt made him one of the town's most eligible bachelors. Witnesses at Martin's trial, few of whom were sympathetic to the Dodds, painted Archie as immature and a bit of a gadfly. One thing was certain — the evidence about to unfold in a Sydney courtroom would blacken his name forever.

* * *

It had been six months — six months of hell, six months of loneliness, six months of torture. And with every day that passed, Catherine Martin was finding it harder to hide the truth. How could she tell her father? It would be the death of him. And Robert, her brother, why, he was likely to do something rash. She had to get in touch with Dodd. Maybe the whole mess could still be put right. Perhaps she could spare them all the shame.

When Henry Forman, the family doctor, called at the Martin house three days before Christmas, Catherine decided the time had come to share her secret. She managed to get a few minutes alone with Forman, and told him she was pregnant with Archibald Dodd's baby. "She told me she had been very foolish herself, but did not charge [Dodd] with any violence," Forman later recalled. Fearing they would be overheard, Catherine passed Forman a note bearing a set of instructions scrawled in ink. "I need to know what his intentions are," she whispered.

Whether he liked it or not, Forman was being entrusted with the role of go-between. "Tell that gentleman," the note read, "it would be better to marry, and for him to let me know on paper how he intends to act, but for God's sake say nothing about it to anyone else. Oh how foolish I have been." She ended the note with a request that Forman meet her in private the following day to deliver Dodd's response.

But if Catherine thought Forman would be her salvation, she was sadly mistaken. The doctor was called away to attend to patients in the countryside over Christmas. Instead of delivering the note, he left it with her father's friend, Edward Archbold, for safekeeping. Forman later swore he did not reveal the note's contents to anyone; Archbold read it but agreed to keep it "a safe and profound secret."

But Catherine was not going to be able to keep her condition secret for much longer. She had been ill off and on since the late summer, and on Christmas Day she had "a violent fit," to use her sister's words. The doctor was summoned, and Forman used the opportunity to tell Catherine he had not conveyed the note to Dodd, and did not intend to. Forman, who exhibited little sympathy for Catherine's plight, probably encouraged her to tell her father. After the doctor left, Martin stayed at his cherished daughter's bedside through the night; at some point, she finally told him the truth.

Martin was devastated. The next morning his other daughter, Mary, found him lying on his bed and "insensible." It took a dousing of cold water to wake him from his stupor. He said nothing to her or his other children about Catherine's condition, but Mary knew something was wrong. For the next five days Martin walked around in a daze, barely eating and sleeping. Friends were startled when he passed them on the street without saying a word, and his haggard appearance and erratic actions prompted some to remark that he must have lost his mind.

Martin became obsessed with saving Catherine's reputation. His first inclination was to take her far away so no one, not even her mother and siblings, would find out she was pregnant. Without explanation, he packed her up on December 27 and headed into Sydney to take a steamer to New York. Mary went along to see them off. But the weather was poor, and the wind so strong that the steamer was unable to enter Sydney Harbour. The ship headed for its next stop without docking.

With that plan foiled, Martin embarked on a new mission — ensuring that Dodd made amends for violating his daughter's honour. The first step was to get the evidence down on paper. Justice of the peace that he was, Martin drafted a formal affidavit in which Catherine described how she had become pregnant. And she told her father exactly what he wanted to hear. She was not a fallen woman; Dodd, she said, had raped her.

It had happened the previous June, she explained as her father used quill and ink to scribble down every sordid detail. She was walking home on the main road from Sydney about dusk when she was overtaken by Dodd, who struck up a conversation. Suddenly, as they passed a path, Dodd seized her and dragged her into the woods. Then he threw her on the ground, undid his trousers, and "while [she] was struggling, raised up her clothes, and did violently and against her consent, perpetrate a rape on her body." Catherine said she screamed for help until she was silenced by a fainting spell. When she came to, she "cried bitterly" and threatened to tell her brother. Dodd, she said, ordered her "to hold her tongue about it so no harm would follow."

Catherine became ill within days, and she attributed the worst of her "fits" to the violence of the attack. Dodd tried to rape her a second time on another occasion, she said, but she managed to fend him off. She swore she had not had sexual intercourse with any other man before or since. To drive home the point,

47

Martin tacked on to the end of the affidavit Catherine's declaration that she was pregnant, and the child's father was Dodd and "no other."

It was an extraordinary document — the sworn statement of a young woman forced to recount the details of her rape to her own father. But was it rape? Was it possible Catherine was too ashamed — or too scared of hurting her father — to admit she had willingly had sex with Dodd? Certainly the pressure to paint Dodd as a fiend, and herself as a hapless victim, must have been intense. And her description of Dodd's sudden, vicious attack seems a bit contrived. But Catherine stuck to her story to the bitter end. Later, when challenged in the courtroom about calling herself "foolish" in the note she gave to Dr. Forman, she said she had been "foolish" for "not telling my father when I was so ill treated."

* * *

Martin had his evidence; it was time to confront the accused. But he was more interested in protecting Catherine's honour than in seeing her attacker punished. First thing the next morning, December 28, he saddled up his horse and headed into Sydney. Dodd was still in bed when Martin burst into the apartment behind his law office. Martin asked Dodd to "make reparation for the wrong" done to his daughter. Dodd's supporters later maintained that Martin was brandishing a large stick as he stood over Archie's bed; Martin denied being armed with anything other than the threat of a rape prosecution. Dodd, intimidated and rattled by the sudden intrusion, agreed to Martin's demand. "If Kate says that I am the father of the child," he said, "I will marry her."

Dodd asked for time to dress and promised to come to the Martin homestead to sort things out. Satisfied for the time being, Martin retreated and headed home. On the way he stopped to pick up his son Robert, who was surprised at how dejected his father looked. "My God," Martin finally blurted out as wagon lurched along the road, "Kate is ruined. She is in the family way by Archie Dodd." Robert listened in disbelief as Martin described his early-morning encounter with Dodd. "The match would be a very bad bargain," was the best observation Robert could muster. Martin agreed, but said he would do anything, even take on the job of Dodd's law clerk, and "soon make a man of him."

By the afternoon it became obvious Dodd had no intention of keeping the appointment, so Martin and his son went back into town. Dodd's office was empty; Martin took a chair in case Dodd returned while Robert tried to track him down. Finding Dodd in a town the size of Sydney proved easy, but getting him aside to discuss a matter of considerable delicacy was not. Robert waited impatiently in the cold as Dodd avoided him by chatting with a succession of lawyers and business associates. Finally, Robert spotted Dodd walking alone on the street and made his move.

"Why have you disappointed us?"

"I'm very busy this morning," was Dodd's lame reply.

"Do you intend to marry my sister?"

"I can't marry your sister," Dodd protested. "I'm engaged to another young lady."

At least that was Robert's description of Dodd's irresponsible approach to the whole affair. But the encounter was likely a lot more tense that Robert cared to admit. For one thing, Robert had taken the precaution of slipping two pistols into his pockets in case the conversation turned nasty. Dodd's attempts to duck Robert could have been prompted by fear rather than by indifference. Catherine, for one, was worried that Robert might do something rash. She had one of her younger brothers carry a note into town beseeching the two men to come home. "If Bob has anything to do with Dodd, and anything unpleasant should take place, I can never get over it," she begged her father. "Mind and secure the pistols from Bob."

Robert reported the gist of the conversation to his father, who was "thunderstruck" by Dodd's refusal to marry. That evening, Martin decided to deal with the matter father to father by making a direct appeal to Judge Dodd. The judge was in his yard when Martin came to the fence and asked for a few moments of his time. Dodd, knowing why he had come, invited Martin inside to a room the judge used as his office. Dodd briefly fumbled through his desk for a match to light the candle, but the two men ended up sitting in the darkness.

"I want your son to make reparation for the wrong he has done my daughter," Martin began.

"I have no control over my son, he is not living in my house," snapped Dodd, who was no happier about the turn of events. "He has given me great dissatisfaction, but he denies the charge made against him."

"He can't deny it. I went to see him this morning, and he said he would meet me to arrange the affair." To Martin's mind, Dodd's initial promise to marry was tantamount to an admission of guilt.

"My son was induced to make that promise under fear of violence," replied Dodd, as the discussion took on a hostile tone.

"I have not used violence. I don't intend to. I've warned Robert not to use violence. I am going to act in a most cool and deliberate manner, and whatever the consequences the law must take its course."

"If my son is the guilty person you speak of," replied Dodd, "I would not walk across the floor to save him from punishment. I recommend you put yourself in a lawyer's hands."

"I intended to take Kate and leave the country, if I could have borrowed the money from my friends. Archie would have never heard about it. Failing that, I went to your son."

"If you had come to me sooner and told me your daughter was ill, I would not have even asked what was wrong," said Dodd. "I would have given you ten, twelve, fifteen pounds to take her out of the country. Until today I never heard my son's name coupled with your daughter's."

"I am afraid it's too late for funds," replied Martin. "The thing has been divulged."

There was nothing left to discuss. Martin left the darkened office and walked home, his mind searching for some way to rescue his daughter from disgrace.

Martin spent part of the following day running around Sydney trying to raise money. Edward Archbold offered to help, but advised against taking anything from the judge. Even though Martin seemed bent on leaving town, he was not giving up on his effort to pressure Dodd into marriage. He asked another friend to deliver a note that could only be interpreted as a challenge to a duel. "Your vile conduct leaves me but one remedy," Martin wrote to Dodd. "Fail me not or I will brand you as a coward."

Edward Bown, who acted as Martin's messenger, was taken aback at Dodd's reaction to the note. "At first he treated it lightly," Bown would later recall. "He told me he was guilty, but not to the extent charged by Mr. Martin." Dodd admitted having "improper intimacy" with Catherine, but claimed another man was the father of the baby. He asked for an hour to consult a friend — possibly his father — before drafting a reply. When Bown returned, Dodd handed him a scrap of blue writing paper bearing his terse reply. "As I am not aware that my conduct toward you has been vile as you have stated," the note read, "I would rather, before giving you the satisfaction you demand, have from you in writing the manner and way my conduct has been so." It was a stalling tactic, and Bown warned that it would not wash with Martin. "Last year I lectured on the rights of women," Dodd noted sarcastically as Bown headed for the door. "This year I will have to lecture on their wrongs."

When he saw the note and heard about Dodd's flippant response, Martin was furious. "He was in a state of great excitement," noted Bown, who felt Martin "had no control over his own actions." That night he came into Robert's bedroom with more bad news — a neighbour had just told him that word of Catherine's pregnancy was all over town. That was not surprising, considering that for days Martin had told almost everyone he encountered that Dodd had violated his daughter. "We will be happy yet," Martin vowed.

The next morning, December 30, Martin was again at his son's door. He was heading into Sydney and wanted to borrow a set of pistols. Robert, who had heard gossip that Dodd was armed, handed them over so his father could protect himself. Within hours Dodd was dead and Martin was facing the gallows.

* * *

The formal investigation into Dodd's murder began at the Sydney courthouse on New Year's Eve. Martin was still in sorry shape, and the lengthy hearing had to be delayed several times over the next few days because Martin was too ill to attend. At one point testimony was cut short when Martin had a seizure and collapsed on the floor. At the outset Martin was without a lawyer despite the seriousness of the charge against him. Whether out of solidarity for a fallen comrade or fear of offending Judge Dodd, none of the handful of lawyers practising in Sydney would take the case. But by the time the hearing resumed on January 3, 1854 — two days after hundreds attended Archibald Dodd's funeral —a rookie lawyer had come forward to handle Martin's defence.

Judge Dodd, who had a murder to avenge and his son's reputation to protect, had no trouble enlisting legal help. He sat through the entire proceeding with James McLeod, a Sydney lawyer and member of the legislature. Dodd was a judge of Nova Scotia's highest court, and the two magistrates conducting the inquest were not willing to challenge his right to seek the truth. Dodd and McLeod peppered the witnesses with questions to make sure nothing that painted Martin and his daughter in a bad light was overlooked. When the magistrates were finished examining Archbold, for instance, Dodd inquired about his conversation with Martin shortly before the shooting. Martin had been raving about his treatment at the hands of the Dodds, Archbold admitted, and had described himself as "God's agent on earth to destroy that fellow." Archbold was not sure which Dodd he had been talking about. The judge also did some sleuthing, convincing Forman to hand over the note in which Catherine chastised herself for being "foolish." It was duly entered as evidence.

Martin was in rough shape, but he was not oblivious to Dodd's presence, or his intentions. The hearing was the first time the two had seen each other since their tense discussion in the judge's office. At one point, probably during a break as he was being returned to his cell, Martin confronted Dodd. "If you, sir, had acted like a father, this dreadful occurrence would not have taken place," he charged. Dodd let the remark pass without comment. To Dodd's mind, shooting a man in the back was as cowardly as shooting a bird before it could take flight. He would get his revenge by making sure Martin did not escape justice. Even without Dodd's intervention, there was more than enough evidence to send Martin to trial. On January 4, after hearing from eight witnesses, the magistrates ordered Martin held in custody until the spring sitting of the Supreme Court.

Martin spent the next six months in the county jail, too sick to eat anything but oatmeal and eggs. And he suffered more seizures. His eldest daughter, Mary, came to his cell daily to look after him. Out of deference to Martin's place in the community he was locked up in a cell usually reserved for debtors, away from the common criminals. Once spring weather came, he was allowed to take short walks around the jail yard.

Martin's case cleared the grand jury on June 6, 1854. Grand juries, which continued to operate in Nova Scotia until the 1980s, served as an extra check on the power of the state. It was the grand jury's duty to hear the outline of the Crown's case and decide whether to deliver a "true bill," sending the accused to trial as charged. The jury had the option of delivering "no bill" — a rare occurrence — ending the prosecution in its tracks. In Martin's case, the grand jurors heard evidence from a handful of witnesses before returning a true bill on the murder charge.

Then the process ground to a halt. The trial was supposed to begin the following day, but Solicitor General William Henry, who had arrived from Halifax to conduct the prosecution, was too sick to attend court. Charles Harrington, an Arichat lawyer assisting the prosecution, was not prepared to handle the trial alone. By June 8, with Henry still confined to bed, it was obvious that there was not enough time left in the court session to fit in Martin's lengthy trial.

Defence lawyer Martin Wilkins, a prominent Pictou County politician who had taken the case in part because of his friendship with Martin, launched an offensive. He argued a delay would be costly — Martin's health had deteriorated during his confinement, and defence witnesses had been assembled for the trial at great expense. And, Wilkins asserted, Martin had "a good and available legal and just defence" that could lead to an acquittal. The bottom line was that Martin should be released on bail to await trial. Martin filed an affidavit with the court declaring he was "unable to endure further imprisonment without manifest danger to his life." Martin's doctor and jailor agreed that confinement was taking its toll on Martin's fragile health.

The presiding judge, William DesBarres, had the final say. He readily agreed to the Crown's request to delay the trial, but balked at the idea of freeing Martin. He could find no precedent for granting bail to an accused murderer after a grand jury had found there was enough evidence to warrant a trial. DesBarres offered Martin some solace, promising to return to Sydney within two months to conduct the trial at a special session of the court.

* * *

The case of *Her Majesty the Queen versus Nicholas H. Martin* finally went to trial on August 10, 1854. It was an extraordinarily lengthy trial for the time — testimony and closing arguments stretched over eight days, with only one break to observe the Sabbath. Thirty-seven witnesses were called, almost half to testify in Martin's defence. The case drew enormous interest in Sydney and beyond. The courthouse, stuffy with the summer's heat, was packed each day. For those unable to get a seat, the weekly *Cape Breton News* suspended its normal diet of war news from the Crimea to provide a complete rundown of the evidence. Testimony filled column after column of the paper over a three-week period, continuing to appear long after the verdict was known.

DesBarres, his long grey beard hanging to his chest, could be forgiven for feeling awkward as he took his place on the bench. He had been appointed to the Supreme Court in 1848, a scant nine months after Dodd, and now he was presiding over the trial of the man who killed Dodd's son. DesBarres had close ties to Cape Breton — his grandfather had been the island's first governor — but there's no evidence he was particularly close to Dodd. Even if he were, he had a reputation for leaving his personal life at the courtroom door. Years later, Desbarres would be remembered fondly as "kind-hearted and considerate ... a man of the highest honour and of incorruptible judicial intergrity." More than anything, DesBarres was simply grateful to have made it back to Sydney alive. Shortly after adjourning Martin's case in June, he had narrowly escaped death when a small sailboat sank while ferrying him across the Bras d'Or Lakes. DesBarres managed to cling to the wreckage until help arrived but another passenger, a Sydney lawyer accompanying him to court, drowned in the mishap.

Solicitor General Henry, recovered from his illness, presented the Crown's case. Eyewitness accounts of how Martin gunned down Archie Dodd were repeated for the benefit of the jury. Wilkins showed the defence's hand early — when it was his turn to question Crown witnesses, he hammered away at how distraught and irrational Martin had been in the days leading up to the shooting. Wilkins was mounting two separate, but overlapping, lines of defence. On one hand, he endeavoured to show Martin was insane at the time of the slaying. Failing that, he hoped the "fearful catalogue of provocations" committed against Martin would encourage the jurors, as he put it, "to take the law into their own hands, as always happens in the case of homicide by duelling, and acquit him." Wilkins expanded on the insanity theme once the defence opened its case on the trial's third day. At the defence lawyer's prompting, Doctor Forman launched into a lengthy lecture on what medical science then termed "homicidal monomania," a form of insanity in which a

Martin Wilkins, an outspoken politician and lawyer, championed Nicholas Martin's cause in court and in the legislature. (PANS/ Photograph Collection)

person affected is "irresistibly impelled to kill." In his doctor's opinion, Martin was "unsound in mind" when he killed Dodd.

It was August 15, the trial's fifth day, before Wilkins called the witness everyone had been waiting to hear — Catherine Martin. Nothing was said about the baby in newspaper accounts of the trial, but Dodd's child must have been born sometime during the previous March. Now, to help save her father from the gallows, she would have to endure public confirmation of her unwed motherhood. Catherine was shown her affidavit charging Dodd with rape, which was then read into the court record. Wilkins, who wanted only to establish the basis for Martin's violent outburst, had no further questions. But on cross-examination, Henry put Catherine's reputation on trial. Had she ever made "indecent overtures" to her father's friend, Charles McAlpine? Was it true that she once spent the night at a local house of ill-repute? Had she not been seen in the company of soldiers from the local garrison? Despite the onslaught, Catherine firmly denied each allegation.

But Henry had only begun his attack on her character. After the defence closed its case, he took the unusual step of calling more Crown witnesses to rebut Catherine's testimony. A succession of witnesses claimed Catherine had been keeping company with soldiers for several years, in particular a certain John Bird of the 42nd Regiment. Bird himself could not be called to testify — the entire Sydney garrison had recently been shipped out to bolster British forces in the Crimea. On cross-examination, Wilkins methodically undermined the evidence of each witness. Incredibly, one man turned out to be an army deserter who was now living with Judge Dodd. Another witness, a woman, was a former Sydney bootlegger whom Wilkins accused of taking money in exchange for her testimony.

Undaunted, Henry forged ahead with his effort to impeach Catherine Martin. Judge Dodd, who had outlined his dealings with Martin at the outset of the trial, was put back on the witness stand. Once, while walking in the woods, he testified, he had spied Catherine "larking" with a soldier. "The one was chasing the other," he said, sounding as if he were still offended by the sight. "They were laughing immoderately." McAlpine, who witnessed Dodd's killing, was recalled as well. During a visit to his parents' house the previous summer, McAlpine said, Catherine had made what he considered "indecent overtures" to him, "in actions" rather than words. The message to the jurors was clear — no proper young lady would openly flirt with a man.

Henry closed the Crown's case a second time, only to find that the defence had a trump card to play. Wilkins had some rebuttal evidence of his own, and called Sydney's jailor, Richard Logue, to muddy the waters. Logue testified that a local woman named Coolan "was so much like Kate Martin, in dress and appearance, that I myself once mistook the one for the other at a distance."

After six days of revelation and character assassination, all the evidence was in. Wilkins and Henry needed a full day to sum up their cases; it took DesBarres another day to review the evidence and the law. Finally, at five o'clock on August 18, the weary jurors filed out to begin their deliberations. Two hours later, with no break for dinner, they returned with a verdict.

Sydney residents who were lucky enough to get seats in the courtroom left no doubt whose side they were on once the verdict was announced. The foreman had barely got out the words "not guilty" when he was drowned out by cheers and applause. After DesBarres restored order, the solicitor general proposed that the jurors be asked the ground for the acquittal — an unusual move to close out an unusual trial. Wilkins protested that the verdict had been properly recorded and the case was no longer in the jury's hands. But DesBarres wanted to satisfy his curiosity, and the defence lawyer reluctantly agreed. Wilkins later claimed only "some" jurors said they found Martin not guilty by reason of insanity; the judge, however, recorded it as a unanimous verdict. Wilkins sputtered that the court "had no right to order a sane man to be detained in custody on the ground of insanity," but DesBarres was unmoved. He ordered Martin to remain in jail until the government decided his fate. The final verdict would be decided in the corridors of power in Halifax.

* * *

Feelings ran high in the wake of the trial, not the least because of the uncertainty surrounding the verdict. The courtroom outburst certainly showed public opinion was on Martin's side in his hometown. And he was attracting a growing number of supporters among opposition politicians eager for new ammunition to use against the solicitor general and his government colleagues. No detail, it seemed, was too trivial to escape the wrath of Martin's sympathizers. The *Cape Breton News* was even taken to task for the way it reported the names of the jurors in one of its accounts of the trial; conspiracy-minded readers accused the paper of intentionally shunting the names of Irish jurors to the end of the list. On September 4, a scant two weeks after the trial, a Halifax newspaper allied with the opposition confidently reported that "the warrant for Mr. Martin's release only awaits the signature of the governor."

But the government was unsure what to do with Martin. While there was a statute dealing with the criminally insane in Britain, none yet existed in Nova Scotia. Nevertheless, it appeared the government was entitled to detain, for an indefinite period, someone found criminally insane. The chief justice, Brenton Halliburton, took that view when the government sought his advice. And there was another factor to consider — Judge Dodd took the liberty of sending a letter to the governor saying he feared for his life if his son's killer were set free. As William Young, the premier and attorney general, later put it, the government was caught in "a most delicate and painful position." Faced with evidence suggesting Martin was dangerous as well as insane, Young elected to leave him behind bars.

Stymied at the political level, Martin's lawyers filed a writ of *habeas corpus* to have his detention declared illegal. The motion, demanding Martin's immediate release, came before the Supreme Court in Halifax in late November. There was no separate appeal court in those days, so Martin's case posed some problems. Dodd was obviously barred from taking part, but it's impossible to say what influence he might have had behind the scenes with his judicial colleagues. Wilkins, for one, suspected the judges were sympathetic to Dodd's plight. But there was nothing to keep DesBarres from hearing the motion, even though his conduct was under fire. Under the prevailing rules, judges were free to take part in appeals arising from their own trials.

Wilkins worked feverishly in the days leading up to the hearing to gather evidence. He filed an affidavit outlining the circumstances surrounding the verdict, and contending that Sydney's sheriff could not produce a valid warrant to support Martin's detention. The ubiquitous Doctor Forman claimed that since the trial Martin had "continued to be perfectly sane and in his right mind, without any symptom of mental alienation." In his opinion, Martin no longer needed to be locked up to protect the public. But the most startling documents put before the court were affidavits from from four of the twelve jurors, including foreman Paul Murphy, contending that their verdict had been an "unconditional" not guilty. What's more, three of the four denied that DesBarres asked them the reason for the acquittal in the confusion that followed the verdict.

Martin's defenders were trying to have it three ways. The Supreme Court was being asked to free Martin because he had been acquitted of murder. If that assertion failed, there was no valid warrant to keep him in jail. And if the court felt not guilty by reason of insanity was the proper verdict, Martin should be released because he was now sane. Those were the arguments Samuel Fairbanks, a prominent lawyer and one of Wilkins' political allies, carried into court on November 26, 1854. The reception was hostile. The chief justice, Halliburton, immediately turned the floor over to DesBarres, who stuck to his guns. The foreman had clearly said the acquittal was based on insanity, DesBarres maintained, "and most of the other jurors gave the same answer, none of them expressing their dissent."

With the first argument dead in the water, each judge in turn offered his views on the case. The chief justice acknowledged that there was no statute on the books in Nova Scotia dealing with the criminally insane, but argued the common law empowered the government to detain people acquitted by reason of insanity. "It would be monstrous of the government had no power to keep a prisoner in custody in such circumstances," Mr. Justice William Bliss added. "If not, a raving maniac might be let loose on the community." Mr. Justice Thomas Chandler Haliburton, who was on the verge of fleeing the bench to pursue his second career as an author and satirist, warned that the courts would likely face an increasing number of insanity defences in the future. "I think the discharge of the prisoner on the ground of his sanity, when the jury have found him to be insane, would be a precedent dangerous to the peace and security of the community." DesBarres, not surprisingly, made it unanimous. Martin's incarceration was lawful, he said, and any further effort to have him freed should be directed to the government.

* * *

Unfazed by his mauling at the hands of the judges, Wilkins promptly took up their offer. When the legislature's spring session opened a little over a month later, he tabled a petition from Martin and a stack of other documents relating to the case. On February 7, 1855, Wilkins rose in the House of Assembly and launched into a speech outlining his client's long legal ordeal. For Martin, who had been behind bars more than a year, it was his last hope for freedom. But for Wilkins, a member of the Conservative opposition, it was also a chance to take potshots at the government. Wilkins, a skilled debater, was as at home in the assembly as in the courtroom. While his political and legal colleagues grudgingly acknowledged his skill as a lawyer, many found Wilkins' bombast and eccentric ideas hard to stomach. Wilkins was grossly overweight, leading one wag to dub him Falstaff, after the comic Shakespearean character of similar girth.

As usual, Wilkins took no prisoners. He attacked DesBarres for refusing to set Martin free, and took a swipe at Judge Dodd for spearheading the drive to keep Martin off the streets. But he saved most of his venom for the solicitor general, Henry, whom he accused of conducting a "persecution" rather than a prosecution. The worst sin, he charged, was Henry's use of witnesses drawn from the ranks of "the lowest of the low — perjurers and deserters" to sully the reputation of Martin's daughter.

Henry met the attack head-on, welcoming the chance to publicly refute rumours that had been circulating for months. Wilkins, he charged, had bullied the prosecutors and the judge throughout the trial, just as he was now trying to bully the government. As for his rough treatment of Catherine Martin, Henry said he had warned Wilkins that he had witnesses to contradict her evidence. "If unpleasant disclosures were made," Henry contended, "the learned member himself caused them."

Martin's cause received some high-profile support from the government benches, underlining the divisions caused by the case. "I pity the one father as much as I do the other," said Joseph

Howe, a cabinet minister, "both will wear these scars to the end of their days." Howe had little time for Wilkins — he once dismissed him as a coward and a braggart — but he was sympathetic to Martin's plight. He challenged his fellow politicians to put themselves in Martin's shoes, and ask what they would have done in Martin's situation. "Had I been on that jury," Howe contended, "I would have pronounced him not guilty, as I believe these twelve men did. If they were fathers, and had daughters of their own, if they were men at all, they could not have given, under the circumstances, any other verdict." The government had a duty, he said, to order Martin's release.

That brought Young, the premier and attorney general, to his feet. Faced with an insanity verdict, at least on the official record, the government had a duty to keep Martin in jail, he told the legislature. But given the constant barrage of letters and petitions from Martin and his supporters, the government was ready to wash its hands of the whole affair. "If anything can be done to relieve this gentleman from incarceration with propriety and safety," Young said, "I shall be glad." The debate dragged into the evening, but finally a consensus was reached — a new jury would be empanelled to decide, once and for all, if Martin should be detained as a lunatic or freed as a sane man.

* * *

The government-appointed commission to rule on Martin's sanity opened its hearing in Halifax on March 13, 1855. Martin, who had been brought to the city several days earlier, was escorted into the packed courtroom by a group of opposition politicians. After a round of handshakes with supporters in the gallery, Martin was afforded the courtesy of sitting with his lawyers rather than standing in the prisoner's dock. Despite his constant complaints of ill health, he seemed to have held up well in jail. A newspaper reporter was struck by "his erect and manly bearing," which suggested "a man of high education and sensitive feelings."

After a twelve-member jury was chosen, Attorney General Young pointed out that the hearing would be the first and last of its kind in Nova Scotia. "If Mr. Martin is acquitted now and set at liberty, it will be fortunate for him that the provisions of the English statutes [allowing detention of the criminally insane], which are now being adopted by our Assembly, were not in operation before." The furor unleashed by Martin's case had prompted the government to make sure the law surrounding insanity verdicts would be clear in future trials. The government, Young promised, would refrain from putting Martin on trial for murder a second time. There was no doubt he had killed Archibald Dodd; the only question for this jury was whether he was now sane.

Wilkins, looking a gift horse straight in the mouth, opened his case with a sharp attack on Young for assuming Martin was insane in the first place. Stubborn to a fault, Wilkins was still unwilling to concede his client had been found insane in the first place. Then he turned to the evidence of Martin's present state of mind. Six doctors who had examined Martin since his arrival in Halifax swore he was sane. But none of the physicians displayed any special knowledge of insanity, and their opinions were based more on conventional wisdom than science. "A child will detect an insane person," one doctor claimed. "I could tell from his appearance, his eye, and the expression of his countenance [that] Mr. Martin is now perfectly sane." Young, for his part, simply sought assurances that none of the medical men considered Martin a danger to others if released.

The jurors declined an offer to question Martin themselves. After a few minutes of whispered deliberation in the jury box, the foreman declared that they had found Martin "not insane." There was an outburst of applause in the galleries, and a throng of supporters gathered around Martin as he emerged from the courtroom, a free man for the first time in more than fourteen months. "We sincerely congratulate Mr. Martin's friends in Sydney on the termination of his long and cruel punishment," the editor of the *British North American*, a Halifax newspaper, wrote approvingly, "and trust that he will soon be restored in good health to the bosom of his family."

The law was finished with Martin, but the wounds opened by the killing of Archie Dodd were not easily healed. That became apparent the next time Martin and Judge Dodd crossed paths. Five months after his release, Martin ventured out in public to attend a clergyman's lecture in Sydney. Shortly after Martin took his seat, Judge Dodd and a number of his friends disrupted the speech by rising en masse and leaving the hall. Martin immediately fired off a letter to the minister apologizing for the incident, and seized the chance to defend his conduct. "To my God I appeal that the crime I was charged with never for a moment entered my thoughts," Martin wrote. "Reason left her abode, and I knew nothing of my miserable situation until I found myself inside the walls of a prison." But even if he had killed in a fit of temporary insanity, Martin had no regrets that he had done the right thing. "I feel confident my prayers have been heard. My life has been spared, my health is good, and I sleep quiet and sound without the shadow of the fatal deed ever crossing my thoughts."

The widespread support for Martin, and the favourable response to his release, suggest public opinion tended to side with the father of a wronged woman. For Judge Dodd, it must have been galling to see his son's name dragged through the mud, and his son's killer free to walk the streets of Sydney. He could be forgiven if he felt the justice system he was sworn to uphold had let him down. Dodd remained on the bench another twenty years; a lacklustre judge at the best of times, he was openly ridiculed in the press as old age began to take its toll. He finally retired at seventy-six, three years before his death in 1876.

Martin lived to see his nemesis buried. Despite the incident at the lecture hall, Martin was restored with remarkable speed to his former position as a valued member of the Sydney community. He lived out his days at Sun Lodge, "respected and beloved by all who knew him," according to one observer. In January 1881, almost three decades after he drew a pistol to defend his family's name, Martin died at age eighty-seven.

Part Three

CIVIL WARS

Angus Walters, hoisting one of trophies won by the racing schooner *Bluenose*, took an American magazine to court in 1946 to defend his reputation. (*Chronicle-Herald/Mail-Star* files)

chapter 6

The Skipper's Good Name

The short story featured in the October 1946 issue of *Cosmopolitan* magazine would catch the eye of any Nova Scotian. "The Miracle of Sable Island" was a soppy tale about the rescue of starving ponies from the barren island off the Nova Scotia coast. The magazine promised readers they would find it "unforgettable."

The author was Edmund Gilligan, a rotund, forty-six-year-old former newspaperman. Thanks to a 1960s television sitcom about a group of comic castaways, that surname now brings to mind inept seamanship. But Gilligan had served as a sailor during the First World War and had become fascinated with the lore of the sea. After working for dailies in Boston and New York, and *Time* and *Fortune* magazines, he traded in his wife and his journalistic career to write fiction. With his second wife and their three young children in tow, he moved to an upstate New York farm to pump out short stories and novels about the sea.

"The Miracle of Sable Island" was not distinguished by its attention to detail — the main character, an elderly Lunenburg sea captain, spoke more like a pirate than a South Shore fisherman. But Gilligan raised the ire of one famous Nova Scotian seafarer over something more serious than phonetics. *Cosmopolitan*'s editors had written a blurb introducing the story and its writer, and that's what caused all the fuss.

"Gilligan can't understand why more writers don't turn to the North Atlantic coast country in their search for fiction material," they wrote. "The seafolk of Nova Scotia with their unchanging traditions, their strong religious beliefs and their

rugged physical life fascinate him." Those sweeping generaliza-
tions were enough to make any Bluenoser bristle, but the editors
were more specific: "He tells, for for example, of visiting Lunenburg
recently and inquiring about a well-known sea captain. 'He's
delivering milk,' said a fisherman with scorn and contempt.
'He's lost his ship and he lives ashore delivering milk, and that's
what he deserves. None of us will have anything to do with him.'

"Why, Gilligan asked, did this misfortune come upon the
captain. 'Why?' said the fisherman with rising indignation. 'For
a very good reason. Because he cursed the Lord, that's why!'

"It seems," the editor's note continued, "that the captain took
his schooner, a famous racing ship, on tour through the Great
Lakes. In Chicago a girl sight-seer happened to touch the
schooner's wheel with her hand, and the captain was so enraged
at this violation that he called a curse upon God for permitting it.
The people of Lunenburg will never forgive him. They think it
only just that he is no longer a prosperous sea captain."

The disgraced sea captain was not named, but his identity
was obvious. It could be none other than Angus Walters, who
had skippered *Bluenose* to victory in the international
fishermen's races of the 1920s and 1930s. He had sailed the
famous racing schooner to the Chicago World's Fair in 1933, and
he was the only retired Lunenburg sea captain involved in the
dairy business — as owner, not as a milkman. And as for losing
his vessel, Walters had sold *Bluenose* in 1942 after an unsuccessful
public appeal for money to preserve the schooner.

His reaction to the article can best be gauged from a biog-
raphy written less than a decade later. The *Cosmopolitan* item
"was too much for the doughty salt from the Nova Scotia port,"
author G.J. Gillespie noted. "He was the first to admit that there
had been occasions when he used language foreign to drawing-
room conversation, but when it came to cursing the Lord that
was a different matter."

After reading the *Cosmopolitan* item, Walters went straight to
a lawyer. He sued the magazine for sullying his reputation as a
skilled and respected sailor. Angus Walters had soundly
thrashed the Americans in five racing competitions; he was

coming out of retirement to take on the uppity Yanks one more time — in court.

* * *

The names Angus Walters and *Bluenose* are inseparable. He was the only man to ever skipper the sleek schooner. Her moments of glory were his moments of glory. And when captain and vessel headed off to race America's best, they carried with them the burden of defending Nova Scotia's long seafaring tradition.

Bluenose was built specifically to restore the province's pride in that legacy — a legacy tarnished in the fall of 1920, in the first race for the North Atlantic Fisherman's International Trophy. W.H. Dennis, publisher of *The Halifax Herald*, and a group of Halifax businessmen had sponsored the competition in response to the America's Cup races. Those races, they felt, were nothing more than a Sunday outing between wealthy yachtsmen, marked more by bickering and underhanded tactics than seamanship. The fisherman's international races were run between Canadian and American fishing schooners — real sailing vessels manned by men who had earned their sea legs fishing cod on the Grand Banks.

In the first series of races for the fishermen's cup, the Nova Scotia representative, *Delawana*, lost badly to *Esperanto* out of Gloucester, Massachusetts. Humiliated by the defeat, the Halifax backers of the racing series resolved to win back the trophy for Nova Scotia. During the winter of 1920-21 an amateur naval architect, William J. Roue, was retained to design a schooner to carry Nova Scotia's colours in the next race. On March 26, 1921, the 143-foot *Bluenose* slipped down the ways of the Smith & Rhuland shipyard in Lunenburg, ready for battle.

Walters, a stubby, thirty-nine-year-old captain fishing out of Lunenburg, was chosen to command the new challenger. "Angus Walters and *Bluenose* were something out of the ordinary: a remarkable marriage of vessel and master," writer Silver Donald Cameron noted in a 1984 book chronicling their exploits.

The son of a sea captain, Walters had gone to sea at thirteen as a deckhand, and had earned his master's ticket and command of his first schooner by age twenty-four. He held the record for the largest single catch landed by a Nova Scotia fishing vessel, and was known as a wiley, hard-driving skipper whose sailing skill had more than once saved vessel and crew from a watery grave.

And when it came to racing other vessels into port, Walters was a born competitor. "He was a genius where sailing was concerned," recalled Paul Crouse, a *Bluenose* crewman in the 1930s. Another former crewman put it more bluntly: "Angus was a bugger to carry sail." Walters supervised construction of *Bluenose*, and liked what he saw. "I knew from the beginning she was a winner," he recalled. "I just figured she was a little faster than their best." They, of course, were the Americans. "In those days the Americans were the cock of the walk in everything they did," he noted with disdain. In *Bluenose*, he saw a way to cut them down to size.

Bluenose recaptured the international fishermen's trophy in the fall of 1921, thrashing the Gloucester schooner *Elsie*. The trophy never left Nova Scotia again. *Bluenose* successfully defended the title in 1922 and 1923, but the races were becoming almost as acrimonious as the America's Cup. In fact, *Bluenose* retained the trophy in 1923 only after Walters, stripped of a victory on a technicality, quit the series in a huff and the American challenger refused to take the title by default.

It was eight years before the racing series resumed. In the meantime, despite the legend that *Bluenose* was never beaten, the vessel lost a 1930 race for the Lipton Cup to the Boston schooner *Gertrude L. Thebaud*. But, in races for the international fishermen's trophy the following year, 1931, and in 1938, Walters and *Bluenose* redeemed themselves, defeating *Thebaud* both times.

The 1938 series was to be *Bluenose*'s last brush with glory. Walters, who owned the bulk of the shares in schooner, took her fishing on the Banks and used her to haul freight. The era of the working sailing vessel had passed, and Walters reluctantly retired from the sea. In 1940 he opened a dairy in Lunenburg, but refused to give up on his beloved vessel. When the sheriff seized

70

the schooner to repay a debt owing on her diesel engines, Walters cashed in his life insurance policy and scraped up $7,000 to keep her off the auction block. Walters mounted a drive to preserve *Bluenose* as a piece of Nova Scotia history, but there was little public interest at a time when war raged around the globe. In 1942 he sold her to the West Indies Trading Company, to carry freight between islands in the Caribbean.

"There was a lump in my throat," Walters recalled of the day he cast off *Bluenose's* lines for the last time. "I knew it was good-bye, and she was like part of me. To tell the goddamn truth, when I walked home, I felt like I was coming out of the cemetery." Four years later, on the evening of January 29, 1946, someone tracked down Walters at the Lunenburg curling rink with bad news. *Bluenose* had struck a reef off Haiti and sank. Walters, the man who epitomized the golden age of wooden ships and iron men, wept.

* * *

Just nine months after *Bluenose* was lost, *Cosmopolitan* served up another shock for Walters. Established in 1886, *Cosmopolitan* — *Hearst's International Combined with Cosmopolitan*, to give the magazine's full title — was part of the empire built by newspaper magnate William Randolph Hearst. Based in New York, the magazine circulated worldwide and sold well in the Maritime provinces. More than 2,300 copies of the October 1946 issue, at thirty-five cents a copy, were sold on Nova Scotia newsstands, and several hundred people in the Atlantic region shelled out four dollars a year to subscribe.

The magazine in the 1940s was remarkably similar to the contemporary version, lacking only a provocatively clad model on the cover. Articles in the October 1946 issue were a combination of short fiction, profiles of celebrities like Broadway star Fannie Brice, photo features, and self-help items. A feature on war-torn Germany was contributed by a youthful GI reporter who's still in the journalism business — *60 Minutes* regular Andy

Rooney. The issue's 224 pages were crammed with advertisements for the finer things in life — fancy clothes, liquor, personal-care products, and cars. An ad for Studebaker, strutting the motto, "first by far with a postwar car," depicted the sleek, "daringly different" 1947 models.

But to Walters, the only thing that mattered was the paragraph on page four about the Lunenburg sea captain. Walters retained Halifax lawyer Charles B. Smith, who demanded satisfaction. *Cosmopolitan*'s lawyers responded in May 1947 with an offer: "We would publish a complete retraction along the lines that Capt. Walters was not the one referred to in our former publication, together with some favorable statement about his success at defeating the United States a number of times in sailing races." Also proposed was a payment of $750 to "compensate" Walters "for his expense."

The magazine's proposal would have only added insult to injury, tying Walters's name to the description of a disgraced sea captain for readers who had not already made the connection. And Walters showed what he thought of the $750 payment at the end of July, when his lawyer filed a libel suit with the Nova Scotia Supreme Court. Damages sought totalled a whopping $15,000. The lawsuit claimed Walters had been "held up to ridicule and contempt." The article falsely stated that Walters was scorned by the people of Lunenburg, had been "reduced to delivering milk for a living," and was "guilty of blasphemy." And he had been libelled not only in Nova Scotia, but across Canada and in the United States and Britain, where Walters was "well-known by reason of his former activities as master of the famous racing schooner 'Bluenose'."

The Hearst publishing empire was not exactly shaken to its foundations by the lawsuit. From the start, Smith was given the run-around by *Cosmopolitan*'s lawyers, who failed to return his phone calls when he was in New York on other business. In September, working through lawyers in Halifax, the magazine applied to have the lawsuit thrown out, claiming the Nova Scotia courts lacked jurisdiction. Hearst argued that the magazine was distributed in Nova Scotia by subsidiary companies and an independent wholesale newsdealer, H. H. Marshall Ltd. Following that logic, Hearst Magazines Inc., the defendant named in the lawsuit, was not responsible for publishing the offensive article in the province.

But Mr. Justice John Doull rejected the magazine's bid to derail the lawsuit in a ruling handed down in September 1947. Even if he accepted the argument that others had spread the alleged libel, the judge said, Hearst was still responsible for copies mailed to subscribers. And Nova Scotia was the proper place for resolving the suit, he noted. "In all its elements this seems to be a Nova Scotia case." Doull went on to make two comments that bolstered Walters's cause. The passages that had raised the sea captain's ire were, on their face, libellous. And, he added, "I am probably not going very far when I say that a great many people who would read the words in Nova Scotia would consider that the reference was to the plaintiff [Walters]."

For reasons that remain unclear, Hearst Magazines did nothing more. Faced with the probability that the libel suit would succeed, based on one judge's assessment at least, the company did not bother to file a defence. Walters won by default. On the last day of October, the Supreme Court issued a judgment against Hearst, and a hearing was set for December 12 to determine how much Walters was entitled to receive in damages.

Hearst was informed of the hearing, but did not send a lawyer to contest damages. With the show to himself, Smith called three witnesses. Robert J. Rankin, managing editor of *The Halifax Herald*, testified there was "no doubt" in his mind that most Nova Scotians would have thought Walters was the unidentified captain referred to by *Cosmopolitan*. An official of H. H. Marshall Ltd. provided circulation figures for the magazine in the Maritimes.

Then Walters took the stand. Smith led his client through a thumbnail sketch of his exploits as *Bluenose* captain, including the 1933 Great Lakes tour and a 1935 audience with King George V. Then he turned to the magazine's allegations. Walters denied making a scene because a woman touched *Bluenose*'s wheel in Chicago. "I won't be exaggerating to say that the *Bluenose* was steered more by the passengers, more so by the female sex than the male sex, while we were on Lake Michigan."

Walters, now sixty-six, described his decision to sell *Bluenose* (he had not "lost" the vessel), retire from the sea and open a dairy. "I couldn't attempt the dairy business and look after the vessel too. It was too much for me."

"Previous to reading this article, had anybody informed you that you were held up to scorn and contempt in the Town of Lunenburg?" the lawyer asked.

"What would I do with the milk? The milk wouldn't be much good to me if nobody in Lunenburg had anything to do with me."

"Is there any truth in the allegation you cursed the Lord?"

"I was no saint when I went fishing," Walters admitted, "Not one today ... but I don't think I would stoop so low as to curse the Lord for something he had nothing to do with."

* * *

The task of assessing damages fell to the silver-haired chief justice, Joseph Chisholm, a student of Nova Scotia history who had been top judge for fifteen years. "A kindly soul," recalled one lawyer, "his reasoned application of the law won him the love and respect, not only of the Bar, but of the entire Halifax community."

But in a ruling delivered four days before Christmas, 1947, Chisholm had few kind words for *Cosmopolitan*. The magazine's statements about Walters were "malicious" and "grossly false," he said. At best, Gilligan had made no effort to ascertain whether they were correct; at worst, he had simply made them up.

The judge angrily attacked *Cosmopolitan*'s offer to settle the case for $750 and a retraction. "To say that the plaintiff was not the party referred to," he said, "would only be to add another falsehood to those already published." Despite the harsh words, Chisholm gave Walters only a fraction of the $15,000 sought in the lawsuit. Damages were set at $3,500.

74

Walters' reaction to the outcome of the case is unknown. The libel suit and the ruling against *Cosmopolitan* were covered in detail in the Halifax press, helping to restore any harm done to his image. Well into his seventies Walters still puttered around the dairy, and he came out of retirement in 1957 to pilot a small government vessel from Lunenburg to Lake Superior.

Walters lived to sail on the maiden voyage in 1963 of *Bluenose II*, the replica he had wanted built ever since the original sank. He died August 12, 1968, his reputation intact, his place in history secure.

chapter 7

Fighting for Justice

Annabella Hubert had a beef with the government. And she was not the kind to take no for an answer. By the time the Nova Scotia legislature convened its 1902 session, Hubert was well-known to the staff of Province House in Halifax. She had been a fixture in the building's corridors for two years, constantly begging to see this minister or that backbencher. Sometimes she succeeded in collaring an unfortunate politician, who was forced to listen impatiently as she recited the story of how the government had stolen her land.

A woman in her seventies who had never married, she described herself as a "large landed proprietor." She was from Arichat, a fishing community at the southern tip of Cape Breton Island. But for reasons that were never made clear, she had lost her land. A believer in conspiracy theories, she claimed she had been "robbed" of her property. The culprits, she maintained, were James Longley, the province's attorney general, "and others."

Hubert's animosity toward the government, and the frustration of Province House officials who had dealt with her on umpteen occasions, came to a head on February 28, 1902. The House of Assembly was not in session, but Hubert, armed with a stack of documents, was inside the first of two sets of doors leading to the legislative chamber, trying yet again to interest passing politicians in her plight. According to the legislature's chief messenger, W.W. Payson, Hubert was talking so loudly that he could hear her from inside an adjacent smoking room.

Thomas Robertson, a Shelburne County MLA who had been named Speaker just two weeks earlier, summoned Clifford Marriot, one of the messengers, to his office. "Tell Payson that woman must go out," he demanded. "I can't have her bothering the members." Marriot relayed the order to Payson, who swung into action.

"The Speaker says you must go out," Payson told Hubert.

"How dare you order me out?" she replied. Then, according to Marriot's account, "Payson put his hand on her arm and she went quietly till she reached the hall. She then resisted, and Payson let go immediately." Another messenger, Frank Greenough, recalled that Payson had one hand on her arm, the other on her shoulder, as he led her into the hall.

Marriot returned to the Speaker's office. "Is that woman out?" Robertson asked.

"She is in the hall," Marriot reported.

Robertson summoned Payson, and made it clear he wanted Hubert out of the building, not just out of the vestibule. "Go and put her out," he ordered. With that, Payson ejected Hubert from the premises.

Payson claimed he used no more force than necessary, but Hubert told a different story. "He took me by the shoulders and violently shook me," she charged. "He pushed me and tried to throw me downstairs. He had been drinking. I could smell liquor on his breath. I said to him: 'If you will leave me alone, I will go out.' He did not leave me alone. I was afraid of him." Payson, she said, forced her down the stairway to a landing. "When he went to open the door on Granville Street, I ran out the other way to get rid of him. I was so much afraid of his treatment that I never went there again."

If Payson thought he had seen the last of Hubert, he was sadly mistaken. Two months later, she filed a lawsuit against him claiming $10,000 damages for assault — a small fortune in those days. Unable to convince the politicians to support her quest for justice, Hubert was determined to have her day in court.

* * *

Hubert first began showing up at Province House during the 1901 session. In March of that year, Richmond County MLA Simon Joyce, a backbencher in the Liberal government of Premier George H. Murray, presented a petition on her behalf. House of Assembly records give few details, recording only that the petition concerned "certain lands at Arichat, and other matters, and also having reference to John H. Rheindress, a justice of the peace for the County of Richmond." Given the involvement of the court official, it's likely the land had been seized to settle a debt or cover unpaid taxes.

The petition was referred to the government for consideration and, according to Hubert, initial reaction was favourable. Edward Farrell, a Liberal from the South Shore, told her the attorney general "should lose his position" based on her complaints. Other MLAs promised a select committee to investigate her "serious" charges against the government.

There was even an attempt to settle the dispute quietly. Duncan Finlayson, a second Richmond County MLA, told Hubert near the end of the 1901 session that a man named Hart, apparently the new owner of the Arichat lands, "wants to speak to you and is going to give you back your land." She brusquely informed Finlayson that the land had never belonged to Hart, and refused to see him.

Despite Hubert's optimism, the government took no action. Undaunted, she chose a more direct approach. One morning, as Attorney General Longley sat at his desk in Province House, Hubert stood outside his office and yelled, over and over, "thief, scoundrel, rogue." Longley later claimed he "paid no attention" to her taunts, but the following day she followed him as he walked to a committee meeting. "[She] kept shouting and I told the messenger [Payson] he must preserve order," said Longley. "He just quietly removed her. There seemed to be no difficulty."

Once again, Hubert had a different slant on the incident. She said Longley "incited" Payson to assault her. If she had not

Province House in Halifax was the setting for a simple case of assault that ended up in the Supreme Court of Canada. (Author photo)

grabbed the bannister as Payson removed her, she said, she would have had "a very serious fall backwards downstairs."

In the lawsuit, Hubert claimed she had been "most brutally treated" by Payson during 1901 and 1902, incidents that culminated with the February 28 attack. Hubert maintained she had "a perfect right to attend to her business at the House of Assembly, as she had not the ready money to engage professional aid, nor could she expect anyone to give the constant attendance in this matter as she could do."

Payson, for his part, filed documents denying he had ever assaulted or mistreated the woman. One of the duties of the chief messenger, he pointed out, was "to preserve order and decorum" in the House of Assembly and the adjacent corridors. Payson said Hubert had been creating a disturbance and interferring with MLAs as they went about their business. Besides, he had acted under direct instructions of his boss, the Speaker. As for the February 28 incident, Payson said he "gently laid hands" on Hubert and removed her from Province House "using no more force than was necessary."

A jury would have to decide which version of events should be believed.

* * *

The lawsuit went to trial in Halifax on November 8, 1902. The government backed Payson to the hilt; Attorney General Longley and Arthur Drysdale, a lawyer and Liberal cabinet minister, conducted the defence.

Hubert, the first witness, described her run-ins with Payson and the attorney general in 1901 and 1902. Questioned by Drysdale, she tried to change the subject and began to ramble about her land dispute with the government. "It was with difficulty that the statements of the plaintiff in cross-examination could be understood on account of her rapid utterance," noted the presiding judge, Mr. Justice Robert Weatherbe. "She volunteered many statements not touching on the [assault] issue with respect to her petition, and the subject of that petition, which I was obliged to prevent."

Payson's defence was hampered by the death of a key witness. The Speaker, Robertson, had died suddenly in April 1902 while visiting his brother in South Dakota. Longley and Drysdale had to rely on Payson and the other messengers to verify the Speaker's orders to have Hubert removed from Province House.

For good measure, Longley himself took the witness stand. A former newsman and a prolific writer, Longley was the bad boy of the Liberal cabinet, better at speaking his mind than toeing the party line. He had opposed then-premier W.S. Fielding's drive to repeal Confederation in 1886, and had argued it would be folly for the Liberals to fight the 1891 federal election on a platform advocating free trade with the United States. He was right — the party was soundly defeated. Sarcastic and outspoken, he "never, in private or public, could deny himself of the pleasure of saying a sharp and biting thing," said one observer. Even one of his Liberal colleagues offered the uncharitable assessment that Longley was "conceited, unlovable and un-bearable."

Longley the witness made no bones about his opinion of Hubert. "She was obviously crazy," he testified. "She was in the corridor and around the House of Assembly continually, and became an intolerable nuisance. Talked wildly, loudly, and in an excited state." The attorney general defended Payson's actions. "He just quietly removed her. There seemed to be no difficulty."

In his charge to the jury, Weatherbe said Hubert's claim she was assaulted during 1901 could no longer be considered because of the passage of time. As for the 1902 incident, the judge came down firmly in favour of Hubert. Payson, he told the jurors, could only be justified in forcibly removing the woman from Province House if he were acting on the orders of the Speaker, and while the House was in session. Since the legislature was idle at the time of the incident, Payson "must stand in the same position as any ordinary citizen who commits an assault." The jury retired for a mere ten minutes before ruling that Hubert had been assaulted and awarding her $500 in damages.

* * *

The government refused to give up, appealing the verdict and damage award. "Whether the House is actually sitting or not, during the whole session the Speaker, through his officers, has absolute control of the whole House, and he can direct any offender to be taken into custody," Longley argued when the appeal was heard in January 1903. He cited parliamentary practice in Britain to back up his contention. Weatherbe had also made a mistake in his instructions on damages. "Considering what had taken place, and the circumstances of the alleged assault, the jury should have been directed that it was not a case for substantial damages." Hubert's lawyer, W.F. O'Connor, countered that the damages were reasonable and the woman could not be removed from the premises after she had ceased creating a disturbance. The powers and privileges of the British

Attorney General James Longley, one of the targets
of Annabella Hubert's allegations of wrongdoing,
dismissed the disgruntled Cape Breton woman as
crazy. (PANS/Photograph Collection)

House of Commons, he maintained, were not part of the common law of Canada.

The four judges who heard the appeal handed down a split
decision three months later. A simple case of assault generated a
ruling that filled twenty-eight pages of Nova Scotia's official law
reports, with each judge presenting his own interpretation of a
century of statutes, parliamentary practice and legal precedents.

Chief Justice James McDonald, an elderly Pictou County
Scot who was entering his third decade as the province's top
judge, felt the verdict should be overturned. A review of the
evidence "lead to the inevitable conclusion that the language
used by the Attorney General to describe the conduct of the

plaintiff, while frequenting the precincts of the House, is not in any degree exaggerated." British practice prevailed, he ruled, and the Speaker had authority to order Hubert removed even though the House was not in session. Mr. Justice Wallace Graham, one of the brightest lights on the Nova Scotia bench, took a similar view, saying a new trial was in order.

Mr. Justice Charles Townshend disagreed. Strip away the rhetoric about parliamentary procedure and the Speaker's authority, he said, and the case became "an ordinary assault." If Hubert was obstructing MLAs and creating a disturbance, "there was a proper way of dealing with her" — meaning, apparently, that Payson could have called in the police. The jury had decided that Payson's actions were not justified, and Townshend could find nothing in the evidence to justify setting aside the verdict. "I cannot help thinking the damages allowed by the jury were very high," he added, but there was "no legal ground for interfering with the sum awarded."

Mr. Justice Nicholas Meagher had the last word. "The plaintiff, it may be said, pursued her claims for redress with overmuch zeal, and exercised a frankness of speech towards the Attorney General not easily borne with, and for which she should then have been removed." But that had happened before the incident at issue in the lawsuit, and served only to show "the manner of woman she was." Meagher upheld the verdict, ruling it had been up to the jury to decide whether Payson's use of force had been justified.

The result was a tie, two judges upholding the verdict, two contending the case must go to trial a second time. It was a rare situation, usually avoided by having panels of odd-numbered judges handle appeals. But, in law as in baseball, a tie goes to the runner. The appeal was dismissed and Hubert's damage award stood.

But the case refused to go away. Payson appealed to the Supreme Court of Canada, which heard the case just before Christmas, 1903. Payson went to Ottawa to argue the case in person, but no doubt he still enjoyed the support of the government. Despite the trifling nature of the assault — Hubert never claimed physical injury at Payson's hands — the fact the incident occurred in Province House raised some weighty legal issues that extended to all Canadian legislatures. Was public access to a legislative assembly building a right or a privilege? Did a Speaker's power to maintain order still exist when the House of Assembly was not is session? Five judges took two months to ponder those questions before handing down a decision. Mr. Justice Louis Davies spoke for the court, ruling public access to the area of a legislative chamber could be "withdrawn or revoked" when necessary "in the interest or order and decorum." The Speaker was empowered to keep order even when the legislature was not sitting, he said, so Payson was justified in removing Hubert if she were causing a disturbance. In Hubert's case, Davies said, the evidence was "overwhelming" that Payson was justified in removing this "excitable and rather erratic person" from the premises. The verdict and $500 damage award were overturned, and a new trial ordered.

Hubert had won some battles, but lost the war. She could have appealed to a higher court — the Judicial Committee of the Privy Council in London was the last word on Canadian cases until 1949 — but no doubt that option was too expensive. As it was, Hubert had lost the will and the money to continue a fight that was doing nothing to help recover her property. She declined to take Payson to trial a second time, and let the matter drop. But the headstrong woman from Arichat had managed to extract her pound of flesh.

Part Four

SPECIAL CASES

chapter 8

Legal Briefs

A Dynamite Love Affair

As a suitor, Thomas Riley was dynamite. Just ask Myrtle Robinson. Or Gilbert Lattimore, Riley's rival for Robinson's affections. Better still, take it from the working-class residents of Halifax's scruffy Albemarle Street who were jolted awake early one spring morning in 1914 by Riley's rather unorthodox way of expressing his emotions.

It was about dawn when Riley, a construction worker, showed up outside Robinson's house at 163 Albemarle Street — now the site of the Halifax Metro Centre. He shouted for Robinson to come out or he would "blow up the place." Hardly the stuff of Romeo and Juliet, but Riley had reason to be riled — Lattimore was on the premises.

Neither Robinson nor Lattimore was eager to make Riley's day. When no one emerged from the house, Riley pulled a stick of dynamite from his pocket, lit the fuse, and tossed it toward an open window. As Riley beat a hasty retreat, the stick landed on the sidewalk in front of the house. Within seconds an explosion chewed up the front of the house and shattered hundreds of panes of glass in surrounding homes and factories.

"A unique way to woo a woman," one of the local papers snickered, free to mock the affair since, miraculously, no one was hurt. But the Halifax police had another term for it — attempted murder. But Lattimore, the man Riley had allegedly tried to kill, proved a poor Crown witness. At the preliminary hearing, Lattimore admitted he had been at the house, but not to see Robinson — he said he had business with a man named Miller who

A crowd gathered on Halifax's Albemarle Street to survey the damage after Thomas Riley used a stick of dynamite to catch his girlfriend's attention. (*Chronicle-Herald/Mail-Star* files)

lived there. Lattimore testified again at Riley's October 1914 trial, but only after he was arrested for ducking a subpoena and lodged in the county jail.

Lattimore's reluctance to testify, and refusal to acknowledge the love triangle that prompted the bombing, undoubtedly weakened the prosecution's case. Riley, who conducted his own defence, was acquitted. A surprising verdict, given Riley's dangerous actions. But perhaps other factors were at play. Press coverage of the case rarely failed to point out that Lattimore — unlike Riley, Robinson, the judge and the jurors — was black.

Faster Than a Speeding Bullet?

He was not the first Nova Scotian to be charged with speeding, but a man named Barker was the first to have his case go all the way to the province's highest court. In April 1913 the Supreme Court cleared Barker on a charge of zipping along the streets of Pictou in his horseless carriage. The court's ruling failed to record just how fast Barker was travelling when nabbed, but obviously he wasn't hard to catch. In those laid-back days the speed limit inside town limits was "one mile in five minutes." In other words, a sluggish twelve miles an hour.

His defence? A sharp-eyed front-seat driver — Barker's wife — swore under oath that he had not been over the limit. And how could she be certain? Well, instead of enjoying the scenery as it whizzed by, she had been nervously watching the speedometer.

Stubborn as a Lawyer

The case of *Hill versus Warner* took three years to wind its way through the courts in the early 1930s, and occupied the docket of Nova Scotia's highest court for nine days. That was a lot of judicial overtime, considering the subject of the lawsuit was an ox. A four-year-old, red and white ox, to be exact, property of one Isaiah Hill, an octogenarian farmer in the Digby area. The whole legal mess blew up in September 1930 when a local constable — that's Warner — seized the ox to recover $8.50 in unpaid school taxes.

Hill, who hotly denied owing anything, fought back. He hired O.S. Miller, an Annapolis Valley lawyer, who drew up the necessary paperwork to reclaim the ox just hours before it went on the auction block. With the ox back to work on Hill's farm, Miller set his sights on bigger game. "This lawyer was a real individualist. There was no one in the profession just like him," noted R.E. Inglis, a Halifax judge who once poked fun at the ox case in an article published in the *Nova Scotia Historical Quarterly*. It was a polite way of saying that Miller was, well, bull-headed. The kind of lawyer who could write a bluntly worded letter to the chief justice about a case and wind up cited for contempt of court — as Miller once had.

Miller launched a lawsuit seeking damages for the week-long seizure of the ox. Rebuffed after a trial in Digby, Miller appealed to the Supreme Court's full bench in Halifax. After nine days of legal wrangling stretched over an eighteen-month period, Miller won the battle but lost the war; the warrant used to seize the ox was declared invalid, but the court refused to award damages or legal costs.

That left Hill with a legal bill for $329.50, a small fortune by Depression standards. Hill, showing he had learned a thing or two during his long haul through the justice system, took Miller to court and managed to have the bill slashed to $195. Whether Miller managed to collect the entire fee, or had to send a constable to seize the ox a second time, is unknown.

The War of the Williamses

Lieutenant William Williams and his wife, Amy, were among Halifax's first settlers. They were also the first Nova Scotians granted a divorce.

At some point during the harsh first winter after the city's founding in 1749, the lieutenant was called away on duty. Upon his return, he accused his wife of pursuing what he termed an "habitual course of adultery." In May 1750 he petitioned the new colony's only court, Governor Edward Cornwallis and his council, for a divorce.

Three witnesses were called, and all testified that Amy Williams had taken up with Thomas Thomas — proof, at least, that she had a penchant for men with repetitive names. The council had no difficulty concluding Lt. Williams' accusations were true. "The conduct of Amy Williams had been infamous in every respect since she had been in the settlement," it ruled.

But the terms of the split were far from equal. While Lt. Williams was "at liberty to remarry," Amy Williams was forbidden from doing the same during her ex-husband's lifetime. As if that wasn't enough punishment, the all-male council gave her ten days to get out of town.

Lawsuit, Anyone?

Sometime in 1936, as he watched yet another tennis ball drift into his yard, Charles DeYoung decided he had had enough. The Halifax railway employee fought back against his neighbour's clay courts in the law courts, serving legal papers to try to stop the serving of tennis balls.

DeYoung lived in central Halifax, next door to the Central Baptist Church Tennis Club. In one year he claimed to have picked up close to three hundred balls that wandered onto his property. The noise and the dust stirred up by the players only added to DeYoung's aggravation.

DeYoung's nuisance lawsuit against the tennis players went before the Supreme Court in January 1939. DeYoung was seeking $500 in damages from the trustees of the church and an injunction to shut down the tennis club. But the fence surrounding the courts was the required height, witnesses pointed out, and great pains had been taken to act on DeYoung's complaints.

It was up to Mr. Justice John S. Smiley to play umpire. After mulling over the evidence for four months, the rookie judge awarded DeYoung $100 for the annoyance caused by errant tennis balls. But he refused to put an end to church-sponsored tennis, saying he found "the physical injury to the land and premises [of DeYoung] too trifling."

As for the noise, the judge felt the "strained relations" between the neighbours caused DeYoung to take "an exaggerated view" of that problem. "The game of tennis requires concentration and calmness," Smiley said in defence of the sport. Advantage, tennis players.

The Battle of the Old Town Clock

It's a little known fact that British troops took part in a pitched battle at the height of the American Civil War. The date was April

16, 1863, the battlefield was downtown Halifax, and the enemy — the local citizenry.

After several nights of skirmishes between soldiers and civilians at some of the city's more notorious taverns and brothels, a group of some three hundred soldiers gathered in front of the Town Clock, just below the ramparts of Halifax's Citadel. Wielding sticks, stones and belts, they swept down George Street, breaking windows and beating anyone too slow to escape. Haligonians, arming themselves with anything at hand, launched a counterattack. The outnumbered soldiers retreated to the top of George Street. Wading into a crossfire of stones and bottles, military officers and a squad of special city constables intervened to prevent further violence. Within hours the riot had been defused and the ringleaders rounded up.

Halifax's newspapers, of course, sided with their readers. "This is the first time in the history of Halifax, or any other civilized place," fumed *The Morning Sun*, "that a lawless soldiery attempted to defy the laws of the land, to insult the entire body of citizens, and to ride roughshod over those whom they were sent to assist in defending the colony against the enemies of England." But some of the city's less desirable characters had done their part to incite the soldiers to violence, and for weeks afterward gangs of civilians roughed up any soldier foolish enough to enter the city alone.

The soldiers who instigated the riot were confined to barracks until tensions died down. Assault charges were laid against a number of soldiers and civilians, but most were acquitted for lack of evidence.

That's Drive on the Right, Right?

April 15, 1923, dawned to what one Halifax newspaper called "delightful driving weather." But motorists cranking up their Model Ts, Maxwells and Chevrolets for a Sunday drive had more than spring potholes to worry about. The buzzwords for the day were: "Keep to the right."

As of two o'clock that morning, motorized and horse-drawn traffic on Nova Scotia's roads switched from the left side to the right. The new rule broke with British tradition, but brought the province in line with Germany, France and the United States. New Brunswick and British Columbia had made the switch a year earlier, leaving Prince Edward Island as the only other jurisdiction in North America requiring drivers to keep to the left.

The change made sense, because most cars were being built for right-side driving. But in Nova Scotia, the new rule was expected to have economic benefits as well. Tourism was emerging as a major industry, and it was feared visitors would avoid driving to the province if it remained out of step with the rest of the country. The only opposition came from the operators of Halifax's street railway system, who were forced to shell out some $50,000 to change switches and move doors to the opposite side of each tram car. The transit company, seeking more time to renovate its trams, lobbied to have the changeover delayed until May 1 in the city. But the government refused, sparing drivers the further confusion of a two-week interval of driving on one side in Halifax and another in the rest of the province.

Elaborate steps were taken to make sure everyone broke the left-side driving habit at the same time. The government distributed stickers for car windshields reminding oncoming cars to "Keep to the right," and for days leading up to the changeover many firms incorporated the slogan in advertisements. For good measure, the main front-page headline in The Halifax Herald on April 14 screamed: "BE SURE — TURN TO THE RIGHT — TOMORROW!"

The PR campaign worked. Not a single mishap was reported during the first day the new rule was in effect.

A 1923 newspaper cartoon offered a grim reminder of the dangers of going against the flow after traffic was switched to the right side in Nova Scotia. (*Chronicle-Herald/Mail-Star* files)

Maybe His Job Was to Clean up Grammar

The name James Maggs won't be found in journalism textbooks, but like Nova Scotia's most famous journalist, Joseph Howe, he was once charged with criminal libel. Unlike Howe, though, he was convicted. And unlike Howe, Maggs was a janitor, not a newsman.

A janitor for the *The Halifax Herald*, to be precise, and in 1912 he was charged with libelling a local politician. Word on the street was that Maggs was not the author of the offending article, but was shielding someone higher up in the organization. Perhaps it was someone who actually wrote for the newspaper.

No matter — a jury found him guilty. The judge, calling the libel "a technical breach of the law," gave Maggs a break. He was sentenced to serve fifteen minutes in jail. *The Herald*, far from embarrassed by the misfortune of its employee, gave the story front-page play, claiming the janitor had obtained "publicity that many men vainly strive a lifetime to enjoy."

The Judge Burst the Defendant's Bubble

R.H. Murray, a Halifax county court judge during the 1930s and 1940s, was never one to hold his tongue. One lawyer described Murray as "a friend of humanity who was known for his keen sense of humour." Yeah, right. This was the same man who once described bootleggers as "cattle" who "should be hanged."

So it's not surprising that Murray was not about to compromise the decorum of his court, even in the name of presenting evidence. In March 1939 he heard a lawsuit brought by a New Brunswick firm seeking payment for seventy thousand sticks of bubblegum shipped to a Halifax store. The lawyer for the Halifax merchant, seeking to prove that the gum received was "hard and musty," proposed to call the storeowner's teenage son to the witness stand to demonstrate that it could not be blown into a bubble.

"I question if it is consistent with the dignity of the court to allow blowing bubbles around in here," replied Murray, who denied the request. At least the youth was spared the trouble of proving his credentials as an expert bubble blower.

Forget Mining, Stick To Writing

Thomas Chandler Haliburton, who gave the world the wise-cracking Yankee clock peddlar Sam Slick, was better at writing satire than working his day-job as a judge. As for his business acumen — forget it.

Haliburton, appointed to the Supreme Court in 1841, inherited lands near his native Windsor that were rich in gypsum. During the 1840s he went into a partnership with a man named Songster to quarry the white, powdery mineral. While touring Britain in 1843, Haliburton gave Songster power of attorney to handle his mining affairs. The upshot was Haliburton returned owing £887 from his mining endeavours — a hefty sum, even on a judge's salary. Haliburton sued, but a jury found him responsible for the debt. An appeal was dismissed by his fellow judges.

Slick, of course, was a better businessman than his creator. "Always ax a sixpence more than the price, and then bate it," he once advised, "and when a Bluenose hears that, he thinks he's got a bargain, and bites directly." Now, if he'd only sold gypsum instead of clocks ...

Let's Settle This out of Court

If you've got a beef with a judge's ruling, you launch an appeal, right? Well, when New Brunswick lawyer A.F. Street took exception to Judge John Bliss's ruling during a trial in 1800, they settled the argument by stepping outside the Fredericton courthouse and fighting a duel with pistols. Neither man was hit, but justice was presumably served.

Nova Scotia's lawyers and judges have been just as quick to issue a challenge to a duel in the name of preserving their honour. During the 1820s James W. Johnston, later the province's premier, challenged an opposing lawyer, Charles Fairbanks, to a duel after Fairbanks bad-mouthed Johnston during a trial. Fairbanks fired first and missed; Johnston, lowering his aim, shouted "I will stop you dancing" and shot Fairbanks in the foot.

But when it comes to bad blood between lawyers, nothing compared to the feud between Richard John Uniacke and Sampson Salter Blowers. In 1791 Uniacke, then Nova Scotia's solicitor general, challenged Blowers, the attorney general, to a duel. Uniacke was miffed that Blowers had hired a servant Uniacke had just fired. No duel was fought, but a few years later they again locked horns. This time Blowers, by now the colony's chief justice, issued the challenge. It seems Uniacke, who had succeeded his adversary as attorney general, had punched out one of Blowers' friends on a Halifax street. City officials jumped in before the men could square off.

Uniacke's son was not so lucky. Richard John Uniacke Jr., a lawyer, shot and killed a merchant named William Bowie in a duel fought in Halifax in 1819. Uniacke stood trial for murder and was acquitted. But the stigma of having killed a man in defence of his honour did nothing to hamper the younger Uniacke's legal career — in 1830 he was appointed to the Nova Scotia Supreme Court.

What Are Friends for?

One of Joseph Howe's closest allies in the fight for responsible government in the 1840s was Lawrence O'Connor Doyle. Nova Scotia's first Catholic lawyer, Doyle served as a Liberal MLA between 1832 and 1855. Howe and Doyle had a lot in common. They were the same age — born nine months apart in 1804 — and both enjoyed good debate, good booze and good company. Doyle was one of the wittiest politicians ever to sit in the

97

province's legislature, enlivening debate with a steady stream of inventive one-liners. "Mr. Doyle seldom made a set speech," wrote a biographer, "but he was pithy and laconic in his impromptu replies."

But Doyle's personal circumstances were not so happy. At one point he was openly accused in the press of being drunk in the House of Assembly, an affront he tried to correct by threatening to horse-whip the paper's editor. By the 1850s Doyle, a widower, had to rely on the charity of friends to keep a roof over his head. In 1853, Howe struck a deal with an elderly Halifax woman named Heffernan "to undertake the boarding, lodging and clothing of Mr. Doyle" for £100 a year. She did so for more than two years, but took Howe to court in 1859 for an unpaid balance of £90.

Called to the witness stand, Howe contended he was not personally responsible for Doyle's tab. He had passed the hat among Doyle's friends and had chipped in more than his share; when the group balked at further payments, Howe refused to make up the shortfall out of his own pocket. *The Acadian Recorder*'s account of the short civil trial noted that the arrangement between Heffernan and Howe was "loosely defined" and "liable to misconception." The jury found in Howe's favour.

By this time, though, Doyle was someone else's problem — he had retired from politics and moved to New York to live with his sister. He died there in 1864.

Gunning for the Attorney General's Post

Otto Schwartz Weeks lays claim to one of the shortest stints as Nova Scotia's chief law enforcement officer — a scant 14 months. Sworn in as attorney general in November 1875, Weeks was a superb orator and highly regarded as a lawyer. His troubles stemmed from his extra-curricular activities.

"When sober he was one of the most pompous men you ever saw," recalled one acquaintance. But Weeks was rarely sober enough to be pompous. On top of his alcoholism, Weeks had a penchant for guns that won him few friends. His escapades with firearms were legendary. Weeks once shot at his wife, striking her in the leg with a stray pellet; another time a lawyer who knocked on his door was greeted with a blast that shattered a pane of glass in the transom. Weeks was also reputed to have a dangerous habit of lying on his bed in hotel rooms and, for amusement, firing shots into the ceiling.

Such antics forced the premier of the day, P.C. Hill, to ask Weeks to resign. When Weeks refused, he was fired. Despite his lacklustre performance as attorney general, Weeks was often retained by the government to prosecute major criminal cases. He continued to hold office as the MLA for Guysborough until 1890, two years before his death.

Where There's a Will ...

James Cosman realized that poverty will always be a problem. But the wealthy Meteghan River businessman, who died in 1911, was determined to do something about it. Because of the unique provisions of his will, his legacy will help needy Nova Scotians until the year 2074 and beyond.

Cosman, a widower with no children, built a lumber exporting business worth $600,000 by the time of his death at age seventy-four. The year before he died, Cosman wrote a will directing that annual payments be made to surviving members of his wife's family and a few charities. Upon the death of the last beneficiary named in the will, the estate was to be split evenly between trustees in Nova Scotia and Donegal County, Ireland — his mother's birthplace. By the time that watershed was reached with the death of a Massachusetts heir in 1974, the estate had grown to $1.4 million.

In keeping his Cosman's wishes, the balance was split, leaving $700,000 in the hands of a trio of Nova Scotia trustees. "One-half of the income therefrom shall be used by the Nova

Scotia trustees for the benefit of the poor of Nova Scotia as the trustees see fit," Cosman's will directed. That income, roughly $40,000 a year, has helped finance additions to two nursing homes in Cosman's native Digby County and supports other charities. The will stipulates that the remaining interest earned by the estate be reinvested "and allowed to accumulate for 100 years or longer if necessary to provide an amount to establish hospitals or homes in [every county of] Nova Scotia for the needy, where they may end their days in comfort."

How much will the Nova Scotia half of Cosman's estate be worth in 2074? A conservative estimate at the time of his death was $60 million. But given the uncertainties of inflation and the up-and-down cycle of interest rates, it's anyone's guess how many hospitals or nursing homes can be built by the estate so far into the future.

Part Five

FRONTIER JUSTICE

Hangman's Heyday

T he newcomer emerged from the front door of the darkened house at half past three, right on schedule. He turned up the collar on his dark coat, yanked down a peaked cap to cover the rest of his face, and began walking. Streets turned muddy by the previous day's rain glistened in the harsh moonlight. Despite the hour, he was not alone. His every move was being recorded for posterity by a newsman who had stood vigil in the late-winter cold, waiting for this moment.

The man taking the early morning stroll could have been a tourist, or maybe a travelling salesman, unable to sleep. Only the reporter and a handful of others knew he had come to Windsor in this, the third year of the new century, for only one reason. He was here to kill, and the time was drawing near.

His name was John Robert Radclive. His title, Dominion executioner. Radclive was in town to make sure that Embrid Mesich Zeid, a Lebanese pedlar better known in these parts as Sion Azubally, did not live to see the sun rise on this March morning.

Azubally had been convicted of murder in the shooting death of another pedlar from the Middle East, whose body had been dumped into an abandoned mine at Tennycape, some distance north of Windsor on the Bay of Fundy coast. A jury found Azubally was the killer, and a judge decreed March 18, 1903 as the date for the sentence — death by hanging — to be carried out.

By the time Radclive reached the building that housed Windsor's courthouse and jail, two members of the clergy were already at work in a basement, praying and talking reassuredly with the condemned man in his cell. Radclive set to work in the jail yard, making a last-minute check of the rope and the trap door of the scaffold, the tools of the hangman's trade. The gallows, shielded from prying eyes by a wall and the pre-dawn darkness, had been erected under his supervision over the previous days, specifically for this moment.

At four o'clock, the county sheriff admitted a small knot of people who had shown up at the courthouse — the witnesses, each bearing a pass that entitled them to watch a man die. Hangings had not been public in Nova Scotia for more than fifty years, but some citizens had to be present to make sure the sentence was carried out in accordance with the law. Not that there was any shortage of people willing to watch Radclive carry out his macabre work; in fact, the hanging had been moved ahead from the appointed time of eight o'clock, before a crowd could gather. Large numbers of people from the surrounding countryside were planning to descend on Windsor, and the sheriff was determined to prevent the kind of rowdiness that had marred other executions. That's why the newspaper reporter, acting on a tip, took no chances and staked out Radclive's boarding house. "The execution could not take place without an executioner," he reasoned.

At quarter past four Azubally, decked out in a black suit and clasping a crucifix, marched from his cell to the gallows. Ahead of him walked the sheriff, a doctor, the jailor and the two clergymen; bringing up the rear were Radclive and two guards. The procession mounted a flight of steps to the platform, where Radclive's work began in earnest. He positioned Azubally over the trap door, and secured his legs and hands with straps. One of the priests recited prayers as Radclive looped the noose around Azubally's neck, then drew a black hood over the condemned man's surprisingly calm face.

Then all was silent, except for the priest's low voice intoning a prayer. "God have mercy on your soul" were the last words Azubally heard. That line was the signal, and Radclive pulled the bolt. The trap door parted with a crash, and Azubally's body shot downward, only to be yanked to a sudden stop as the rope snapped taut. If the hangman does his job properly, the force of the drop breaks the neck like a matchstick and death is almost instantaneous. Sloppy executioners have been known to decapitate their clients, or leave them to slowly strangle to death as they struggle helplessly on the end of the rope. But Radclive was a perfectionist, and Azubally was afforded a speedy exit. After fifteen minutes, the doctor declared him dead and the body was cut down and placed in a coffin for burial.

Azubally "exhibited wonderful nerve and fortitude," *The Halifax Herald* assured its readers the next morning. "He never flinched from the time the procession started for the gallows until the drop occurred." Justice had been served in the old fashioned, Old Testament way — an eye for an eye, a tooth for a tooth, a death for a death. The hangman has been out of business in Canada since the early 1960s, but for most of the past two centuries the noose was the ultimate penalty under the criminal law. Who died on the gallows? Who escaped? The rise and fall of capital punishment in Nova Scotia underlines society's changing attitudes toward crime and punishment.

* * *

Nova Scotia's early lawmakers could hardly be accused of being soft on criminals. In the late 1700s some two dozen crimes were punishable by death. Not surprisingly, big-time offences like murder, treason, rape, manslaughter, arson and highway robbery could bring a one-way trip to the gallows. But also on the list of capital offences were crimes that could hardly be classed as heinous — polygamy, major theft, maliciously firing a gun, cutting a hole in a dyke to cause flooding, and impersonating another person at a bail hearing. First offenders convicted of some of the less-serious capital offences could look forward to a respite of sorts — branding of a letter on the thumb. In the days before criminal records were kept, the brand made it impossible for a repeat offender to escape the full weight of the law.

Conviction for non-capital crimes was no cakewalk, either. Thieves, fences, forgers, counterfeiters and the like could be sentenced to be flogged in public or to spend time in the pillory. People convicted of lying in court were liable to have their ears nailed to the pillory. And some crimes could draw banishment to Bermuda or Australia, which were a far cry from the popular tourist destinations they are today.

The depths of state-sanctioned cruelty was in keeping with an era when life was harsh, short and cheap. The law was designed to mete out punishment that was swift and severe. It was one way for the ruling class to keep the riff-raff in their place — eliminating those found guilty, and intimidating others who might be contemplating similar crimes. The Royal Navy certainly knew how to keep its unruly sailors in line. British seamen convicted of mutiny or piracy were sometimes hanged from the yardarms of their vessels, their tarred bodies strung up near the entrance to Halifax Harbour as a blunt warning to others. One Nova Scotia judge underlined the dual purpose of capital punishment in the late eighteenth century, when he passed the death sentence on two men convicted of murder. "What alone remains for me is to pronounce that sentence which the law has appointed for crime like yours — a sentence full of horror ... a terror to evildoers, and a security to them that do well."

That philosophy extended to crimes that would be considered trifling today, and in the early years judges were not adverse to imposing the death sentence in such cases. During 1785 a dozen criminals were hanged in Halifax alone, one a man who had stolen potatoes, presumably for food rather than profit. Brittain Murray was executed in 1786 at Shelburne for a burglary; a year later, two men were hanged in the district of Argyle at western end of the province for killing sheep and cattle.

But by the early years of the nineteenth century new attitudes to punishment were emerging. Even though the death penalty remained on the books for relatively minor crimes, there were ways to temper justice with mercy. Judges had the power to recommend leniency or pardons, and that option became a means of preventing the unfortunate and the unlucky from swinging on the gallows along with hardened criminals. The colonial government, which had the final say over who lived and died, was usually quick to accept such recommendations. By the 1830s a commission set up to recommend legal reforms noted, apparently with no pun intended, that the death penalty attached to most crimes was "a dead letter" and should be repealed.

* * *

Serious crimes like murder, piracy, mutiny and treason survived as hanging offences. And the public's thirst for retribution was insatiable. Newspapers featured lengthy, often lurid accounts of murder trials and the resulting hangings, sparing few details of an offender's last moments. Capital punishment was even used as an advertising vehicle. "A Hangman Wanted," declared an eye-catching item in an 1884 issue of a Halifax newspaper; it turned out to be an advertisement for wallpaper. Large crowds attended hangings, which often took on a festive air. Executions were considered a form of entertainment suitable for children. One woman recalled how, when she was only ten, her father packed up the family in a carriage and battled the crowds to see four men hanged for piracy on the Halifax Commons in the 1840s.

But deterring others from committing crime, not providing free entertainment, was the rationale behind executing offenders in public view. Public hangings were discontinued in the 1860s, but that did not prevent some from satisfying their morbid curiosity. In 1914, people lined up at a Halifax funeral home to glimpse the body of a man executed for murder. But taking executions out of the public eye did not prevent some observers from questioning the traditional way of sending the condemned to their deaths. "Capital punishment is the law of Canada and must be observed," *The Halifax Herald* noted in 1925 after Lewis Marshall Bevis was hanged for murdering a Halifax policeman. "But in this advanced age the law should be so amended as to provide for some more desirable method of carrying out the dictates of the law."

The reason for the second guessing was simple — hanging was a brutal form of execution. Early hangings in Nova Scotia resembled the lynchings of the Old West. In 1790, for instance, a Halifax woman convicted of murder was hanged using a horse-drawn wagon as a platform. But even when a proper gallows was used, an inexperienced or ill-equipped hangman could botch the job. When ship's cook Henry Dowcey was hanged in Halifax 1866 for murdering the captain of his vessel, a misplaced noose "caused a convulsive struggle before death ensued," said one witness. British government officials, seeking to prevent "those shocking accidents which sometimes occur at executions," sent a confidential report to Nova Scotia's provincial secretary in 1880, complete with diagrams and tips on how hangings should be conducted. "The executioner should be a trustworthy and intelligent person," it advised, stating the obvious. The report recommended the executioner use a proper trap door and a strong, dry rope, which was guaranteed to bring about a speedy death "from dislocation of the neck or nervous shock."

Finding someone "trustworthy and intelligent" who was willing to kill people for a living was not as easy as it sounded. There was no shortage of candidates, but the job of hangman sometimes took its toll. According to Thomas H. Raddall in his history of Halifax, the local hangman during the mid-1700s, a man nicknamed "Tomahawk," eventually drank himself to death. Preparations for hangings, everything from erecting the gallows to hiring the hangman, was the responsibility of the local sheriff, an appointed official more accustomed to collecting bad debts and conducting bankruptcy auctions. In rural areas where murders were few and far between, it was tough for the sheriff to find someone with the specialized skills required of a hangman.

After Confederation, the federal government stepped in to solve the problem. At the request of the Ontario government — no doubt in the wake of a bungled execution in that province — Ottawa created the post of Dominion executioner in 1892. For

$700 a year, the executioner was to be available to carry out a death sentence anywhere in Canada.

The federal government did not have to look far for a full-time hangman. J.R. Radclive had served in the Royal Navy before settling down in Toronto as steward at a boat club. While posted on a ship patrolling the coast of China, he had been assigned to hang pirates from the rigging. As far as Radclive was concerned, hanging should be done as swiftly and humanely as possible. In 1890, after hearing about a condemned man who slowly strangled to death on the gallows, Radclive volunteered his services. "I will offer to hang the next man and put a stop to that sort of torture," he vowed. Within two years, the government took him up on the offer.

Radclive plied his trade across the country for twenty years, and his executions numbered in the hundreds. He did not shun publicity, and on at least one occasion spent the night before an execution playing cards with a local newspaper reporter. But his sinister occupation made him an easy target for rumour and innuendo. After the Azubally hanging in Windsor, there were press reports that Radclive had gone on a drinking binge in Saint John, New Brunswick, on his way back to Ontario. A Windsor police officer travelled to Halifax and made a personal call at the newspaper office to refute the reports. Radclive was still in Windsor, he confirmed, "never tasted liquor" during his week-long sojourn in the town, "and has acted in a most gentlemanly way."

Radclive's tenure as Dominion executioner ended just before the outbreak of the First World War. His replacement was another British import, Arthur Bartholomew English. The new hangman preferred to be called Arthur Ellis, and that became the pseudonym for every Canadian executioner who followed in his footsteps.

Alex Campbell of Dartmouth was present for what must have been Ellis's last hanging in Nova Scotia. As a young RCMP constable, he was detailed to witness the March 1935 hanging of Daniel P. Sampson, who stabbed to death two boys who taunted him with racial slurs. "It wasn't any party, it was a sombre affair,"

Gallows erected behind the Halifax jail for the 1935 hanging of Daniel Sampson, one of the last Nova Scotians executed for murder. (PANS/Photograph Collection)

Campbell recalled long after his retirement. The gallows, erected behind Halifax's county jail, was shrouded in burlap to prevent the curious from viewing the execution. "It worked like clock-work," added Campbell. The trap was sprung and the con-demned man's neck snapped with a sound "like a crack of a pistol."

But not all Ellis's executions went so smoothly. While Radclive had been a perfectionist, Ellis had less luck ensuring his charges died of a broken neck rather than slow strangulation. In fact, his hanging days came to an abrupt end not long after the Sampson execution. Ellis misjudged the weight of a woman being hanged for murder, and her head was severed. At seventy-one, Ellis was forced into retirement.

* * *

By the twentieth century, the need for the hangman's grisly services was subsiding, at least in Nova Scotia. Between 1920 and 1949, only seventeen people in the province were convicted of murder and sentenced to death — barely one every two years. Jurors hearing murder cases were well aware that a verdict of guilty would lead to the death sentence, and substituting a verdict of manslaughter was a convenient way of keeping blood off their hands. Even when a murder verdict was returned, juries often tacked on a recommendation that the death sentence be commuted to term of life in prison. Of the seventeen convicted of murder in Nova Scotia in the twenty-nine-year period ending in 1949, seven had their sentences commuted to life in prison.

The decision on whether to send a convicted murderer to the gallows or to prison was left to the political leaders. After Con-federation, Nova Scotians found guilty of murder had their cases reviewed by staff of the Department of Justice in Ottawa. Based on their advice, the justice minister would forward a report to the federal cabinet recommending that the death sentence be con-firmed, or a prison term substituted.

111

Despite the gravity of the decision, a flip through the files prepared in a number of Nova Scotia murder cases shows the review was an informal process. The Justice Department usually asked the judge who presided at trial what he thought should be done, and doctors were routinely dispatched to examine the convict. Sometimes a transcript of the trial would be examined to assess the evidence of guilt, sometimes not. The biggest factor seemed to be the reaction of the local community. Many murderers were spared after clergy and other community leaders mounted petition drives asking that the death sentence be commuted.

Since a convicted murderer's survival often boiled down to a popularity contest, the poor and members of minorities often bore the brunt of capital punishment. Race has long been cited as a factor in executions in the United States, where statistics show blacks are more likely to die than whites. But the Nova Scotia experience has been less clear-cut. Between 1930 and 1937 nine men — six white and three black — were handed the death sentence for murder in the province. Four of the whites were executed, while two of the blacks died on the gallows. One of the blacks, Everett Farmer of Shelburne, bears the dubious distinction of being the last person executed in Nova Scotia. He was hanged for murdering his half-brother in 1937.

chapter 10

First Blood

Nationality might have had something to do with it. After all, the French and the English had just ended the latest round in their interminable wars. Whatever the reason, there was bad blood between Peter Cartcel and Abraham Goodsides.

Cartcel stood out like a sore thumb among the settlers, soldiers and sailors who had braved the voyage from England in the summer of 1749. There was a smattering of Irish, Scots and Germans among the thousands sent to carve out a foothold on Nova Scotia's wild, rocky shores, but the new settlement — Halifax, it would be called — was to be a predominantly English settlement. But there he was, Peter Cartcel, a Frenchman who spoke little or no English, among the crew of the square-rigger *Baltimore*.

Goodsides was boatswain's mate on *Beaufort*, another ship that had carried settlers to this remote corner of His Majesty's sprawling empire. Goodsides was English, but he apparently understood some French. Enough, at least, to spot an insult.

It happened in a flash on the afternoon of August 26. As one witness later recalled, Cartcel and Goodsides were talking on board *Beaufort* when Goodsides asked why the Frenchman "used him ill." Cartcel replied in French. None of the onlookers understood what was said, but the meaning was not lost on Goodsides. He challenged Cartcel to a fight, and slapped him across the face for good measure.

Cartcel's reaction was as swift as it was deadly. He thrust a four-inch knife into Goodsides' chest, burying it to the hilt. "I am gone!" Goodsides cried out; he was dead before his body crumpled onto the wooden deck. Hands reached out to grab Cartcel, but he managed to wound two other men before he was cornered and overpowered.

* * *

Halifax boasted only a few wharves, a sawmill and a warehouse when Goodsides met his untimely demise. On shore, the thick forest was slowly giving way to the axe, but only about twenty acres had been cleared at the planned townsite. The city about to rise from the wilderness would be named for Lord Halifax, the British colonial official who wanted an instant English settlement to offset the powerful French bastion at Louisbourg. But by late August, Halifax was still a floating city; a dozen ships were crammed with about 2,500 settlers, waiting out the summer heat until accommodations were available on shore. It was the kind of cramped, uncomfortable conditions that could make tempers flare. And maybe, in the heat of the moment, turn a simple argument into murder.

Cartcel's violent outburst was just one more headache for Edward Cornwallis, the career British soldier who was struggling to get houses and pallisades built before winter closed in. Cornwallis, barely thirty-six, had been chosen as Nova Scotia's new governor by virtue of his family's political connections in the court of King George II. As governor, Cornwallis was given sweeping powers to "erect, constitute and establish such and so many courts" as he deemed necessary, and to choose and swear in judges. Not surprisingly, a military man with no legal background like Cornwallis fell back on tradition to create a justice system from scratch. Since 1721, justice in Nova Scotia had been meted out by the governor and an appointed council, sitting in the former colonial capital of Annapolis Royal. Cornwallis followed suit, naming six of the new settlement's most prominent men to a council to handle the business of government. He and the six councillors would collectively dispense justice as something called the "general court." Some might argue Cornwallis's do-it-yourself justice system had at least one advantage — there were no lawyers.

* * *

The King versus Cartcel, the first murder case tried under English law in what would later become Canada, proceeded at a brisk pace. Two days after Goodsides died, the general court met and decided to put Cartcel on trial without delay. Within five days of the murder, court convened in the warehouse. In accordance with English procedure, the facts were outlined for a grand jury, which returned an indictment for murder. The lengthy, rambling indictment charged that Cartcel, "not having the fear of God before his eyes, but moved and seduced by the instigation of the devil," had "most traytorously [sic] and voluntarily killed and murdered against the peace, crown and dignity of our sovereign the King."

Cartcel was brought before the court to enter a plea. Speaking in French, Cartcel asked the court to supply an interpreter. One was assigned, and conveyed Cartcel's plea of not guilty to the charge. A twelve-man jury was then empanelled to hear the witnesses. The jurors represented a cross-section of Halifax's first settlers — the eleven who can be identified from passenger lists included four sailors, a surgeon, a schoolmaster, three farmers and two artisans. One had crossed the Atlantic on the same ship as Goodsides; none had come over with Cartcel. The method used to select the jurors is unknown, but the prisoner apparently had no say in who would decide his fate.

There were only four witnesses. Three sailors testified in succession, giving similar accounts of the brief argument and sudden stabbing. All described how a slap on the face had been answered with a swift jab from Cartcel's knife. But their testimony may have been coloured against Cartcel — the death occurred on Goodsides' ship, and they were presumably shipmates of the dead man. The final witness, though, had no ob-

115

vious axe to grind. Roger Snowden, a constable, described a dispute that had erupted between the two men earlier the same day.

Cartcel questioned none of the witnesses to challenge their version of events. When the witnesses finished, Cartcel announced through his interpreter that he had no evidence to call. Two centuries later, Cartcel's predicament would deeply trouble Joseph Chisholm, Nova Scotia's chief justice in the 1930s and 1940s and an amateur legal historian. He felt the court should have provided Cartcel with an advocate — an educated layman at least, since there seemed to be no one in Halifax with formal legal training. "The prisoner was a foreigner, probably friendless, ignorant of the language of the court, and without anyone to cross-examine the witnesses or speak a word in his defence," Chisholm pleaded belatedly on Cartcel's behalf.

The jury retired for half an hour before declaring Cartcel guilty as charged. Asked if he had anything to say before sentence was passed, Cartcel simply requested the only privilege extended to those condemned to die — a clergyman. Cornwallis, in his dual role as governor and president of the court, ordered Cartcel to hang. There was little time for Cartcel to seek solace and forgiveness with a priest — the sentence was carried out in two days. Cartcel was charged, tried, convicted and executed within a week of the stabbing.

Cornwallis took pride in how quickly and efficiently the trial had been handled. "We endeavoured to follow as near as possible the English laws and customs," he reported to his bosses back in England. "We may have failed in form, but the substance and design of the law was certainly observed." His superiors detected no flaws in the procedures used. "Your method of proceeding in the trial," officials of the Board of Trade and Plantations assured Cornwallis, "was very regular and proper." And the trial came at a good time, making it abundantly clear that Halifax would be under the rule of law. "It will convince the settlers of the intention of conforming to the laws and constitution of the mother country in every point," the Board of Trade noted. And making the right impression on the ragtag collection of people sent overseas to found Halifax was a major goal of the

Joseph Chisholm, a chief justice of Nova Scotia, questioned the handling of Halifax's first murder case almost two centuries after the verdict. (*Chronicle-Herald/Mail-Star* files)

entire exercise. Cartcel's trial and execution was "almost a show-piece performance," in the words of one legal scholar. "Clearly it was intended to be that as much as a means of punishment."

But the rush to avenge Goodsides's death did not sit well with Chisholm. "A little less haste would not have been to the discredit of the court," he complained in a 1940 article published in the *Canadian Bar Review*. Rather than putting the case to a jury within days of the offence, the trial should have been postponed "until the excitement caused by the homicide and the disturbed feelings of the people had in some degree subsided."

But Chisholm felt Cartcel's trial "fell far short of ideal justice" on a more fundamental level. If Cornwallis and company had indeed tried to adhere "as near as possible" to the laws of England, the outcome of the trial might well have been different. Then, as now, a charge of murder may be reduced to manslaughter if there is evidence of provocation. A person who strikes out at another in the heat of the moment, in response to a threat or affront, may not have intended to kill. In that case, it is open to the jury to substitute a verdict of manslaughter, a crime punishable by a prison sentence rather than death.

What about Cartcel's crime? All the witnesses described the same scene — Goodsides slapped Cartcel across the face and challenged him to a fight; Cartcel lashed out with a knife. The single stab wound caused death instantly. A manslaughter verdict would have been consistent with those facts. "It is not outside the bounds of reason that an impartial jury, properly instructed by the court, would have found that the homicide was committed in the heat of passion," Chisholm contended with the benefit of hindsight. "In fact, it would have been hard for them to have found otherwise."

But the manslaughter option was never put before Cartcel's jury. It's conceivable a court composed of laymen was ignorant of the legal distinction between the two crimes. In their haste to lay down the law in the fledgling settlement, it's likely they did not care.

chapter 11

The Tell Tale Chalk

I t was settled — the two men were going to stay the night. The old farmer would hear of nothing else. And that suited the Boutilier brothers fine. Just fine.

George Boutilier and his younger brother, John, had visited the homestead earlier that brisk March day in 1791, and George Frederick Eminaud was pleased to see they had returned. Eminaud, who had just turned seventy, lived with his wife and granddaughter on First Peninsula, just north of the South Shore settlement of Lunenburg. He appreciated having some male company. Besides, the Boutiliers were more like family than guests.

The elder Boutilier was Eminaud's godson and namesake, so it was not surprising that the brothers, who lived a short distance inland at Northwest, often stopped by. But this would be their last visit. Heading to the barn through the darkness to fetch straw for his guests' bedding, Eminaud never suspected the real reason the Boutiliers had suddenly returned. They had needed some time to summon up their courage for the work that lay ahead.

Eminaud, his arms wrapped around a bundle of straw, was almost to the house when his assailants struck with a hatchet and wooden clubs. He died on the spot. The Boutiliers headed inside and used the hatchet to kill Eminaud's wife. The granddaughter managed to crawl partway out of a window as she tried to escape. She was hauled back inside and hacked to death.

Eminaud was rumoured to keep money on hand, and the Boutiliers sacked the house, greedily snatching everything they could find. They rifled Eminaud's pockets and helped themselves to the contents, even a worthless piece of red chalk. Then the Boutiliers turned to the second phase of their plan. They dragged Eminaud's body inside and set fire to the house in hopes of destroying all evidence of their bloody deed. As flames consumed the house and the bodies of its occupants, the Boutiliers disappeared into the forest, headed eastward. To confuse their trackers, they strapped on their snowshoes backwards.

The glow of the fire could be seen from Lunenburg, but the house had burned to the ground by the time help arrived. Despite their efforts to dispose of the evidence, the Boutiliers had been sloppy. Eminaud's bloodied hat was found on the ground beside two wooden clubs. The reversed tracks in the snow fooled no one. The perpetrators of the crime were headed east, in the direction of Halifax.

It took two days for the news to reach the colonial capital. For a triple murder committed so close to home, the crime commanded surprisingly little interest in the Halifax press. The city's newspapers, stacked with advertisements for everything from dry goods to runaway slaves, devoted most of their remaining space to items, sometimes months old, lifted from British and American papers delivered by ship. *The Weekly Chronicle*, for instance, devoted a single paragraph to the Lunenburg murders, which it termed a "horrid" and "unnatural deed."

But the news, however sketchy, travelled faster than two men slogging through the bush and deep snow. Halifax County's sheriff, a man named Clarke, was on the lookout. On March 24, five days after the murders, he arrested two men, newly arrived from Lunenburg, at a shanty north of the city. It was the Boutilier brothers.

They appeared before a pair of justices of the peace the next day for an interrogation. "We do not learn that anything material transpired which tended to support the opinion of their guilt," *The Chronicle* told its readers. "They are, however, still kept in custody." Unknown to the press, the authorities had come up with a compelling piece of evidence linking the Boutiliers to the crime. It was enough to charge George and John Boutilier with murdering George Eminaud by inflicting "mortal strokes, wounds and bruises ... with certain large sticks and a tomahawk." The two men were jailed in Halifax to await trial.

* * *

The last thing Nova Scotia's understaffed and much-maligned judiciary needed was a major murder trial. The quality of the Supreme Court judges had been under fire for years. Much of the criticism came from Loyalist newcomers eager to snap up judicial posts for themselves, but they had a point. After Chief Justice Bryan Finucane died in 1785, the British were slow to fill the vacancy. That left two assistant judges, Isaac Deschamps and James Brenton, to carry the court's entire workload. Their meagre ranks were stretched even thinner by a rule, in force until the 1830s, requiring two judges — the chief justice and one other judge — to preside over all criminal and civil trials. In other words, Deschamps and Brenton had to handle every trial conducted in the far-flung communities springing up around the colony.

Neither man was up to the task. Deschamps was a former judge of the inferior court of common pleas, the lowest rung on the evolving colonial court structure. Although he had no formal legal training, he was appointed to the Supreme Court in 1770 and took over as chief justice upon Finucane's death. Brenton at least had the legal credentials to be on the bench — he had been a lawyer in his native Rhode Island, and had served stints as Nova Scotia's solicitor general and attorney general. But even though he rose to the rank of the colony's chief law enforcement officer, his legal expertise was suspect. One historian suggested Brenton had been named to the Supreme Court in 1781 "for want of anyone better."

Dissatisfaction with the performance of the two judges boiled over in 1787. The assembly, the colony's elected body, went into a rare secret session to debate the issue and emerged with a demand that Governor John Parr launch an investigation into the judges' behaviour. The governor refused, but the issue continued to fester. In 1790, the assembly voted to impeach both Deschamps and Brenton for what it called "high crimes and misdemeanours." The whole mess was sent overseas for a final decision, and it took another two years for the British authorities to decide that the pair should be allowed to keep their posts. Their shortcomings as judges, if any, were put down to "the frailty of human nature."

But the British took steps to beef up Nova Scotia's courts soon after the assembly went public with its criticisms. Deschamps was shunted aside as chief justice in the summer of 1788 in favour of Jeremy Pemberton. Now here was someone with the law in his blood — grandson of a lord chief justice of England, Cambridge educated, a product of London's inns of court. But Pemberton lasted barely fourteen months as Nova Scotia's top judge. He resigned in the fall of 1789 due to ill health, and died less than a year later. He was forty-nine.

The British tried again, this time opting for someone even younger than Pemberton in an effort to put the colony's justice system back on track. Scottish-born Thomas Andrew Lumisden Strange was thirty-two when he was tapped to become Nova Scotia's sixth chief justice in late 1789. Two centuries later, his gigantic portrait, large as life, stares down over the wood-panelled Halifax courtroom reserved for sittings of the Nova Scotia Court of Appeal. Resplendent in scarlet robes trimmed in silver fur, Strange strikes an imposing figure. But his chest-length grey wig — a legal fashion accessory that never really caught on in Nova Scotia — frames a surprisingly youthful face. It's perhaps ironic that Strange, in portrait, would be condemned to continue presiding over cases long after his death; when he showed up for his new job he was far from comfortable in such surroundings. Strange had "a reputation as an excellent theoretical lawyer," says historian Brian Cuthbertson, "but he had little courtroom experience and he was somewhat unsure of himself." The trial of the Boutilier brothers would be his first major test.

* * *

Thomas Strange, sent to Nova Scotia to clean up the judiciary, faced his first test in 1791 when he presided over a triple murder case in Lunenburg. (*Chronicle-Herald/Mail-Star* files)

In late April 1791, the Royal Navy schooner *Diligent* cast off from a Halifax wharf and and struck a southwesterly course once it cleared the harbour's mouth. On board were two passengers who had a date with the law in Lunenburg, George and John Boutilier. A few days later another navy vessel, the cutter *Alert*, followed bearing Strange and Brenton. As chief justice, Strange would do all the talking once the murder trial got under way. And that was probably fine with Brenton, who was still under the cloud of the assembly's impeachment resolution of the previous year.

Only one account of the three-day murder trial has survived, and hardly an unbiased one at that. Written by James Stewart, a Halifax lawyer and future judge who prosecuted the case, it provides few details of the evidence. But we do know that on May 3, a grand jury heard an outline of the Crown's case and returned a true bill sending the Boutiliers to trial. The following day Stewart delivered his opening address to the trial jury. The evidence against the two accused was "purely circumstantial," he admitted, "but after fullest consideration [it] had left in his mind a violent presumption that a murder had been committed." He hoped the jurors would draw the same "violent presumption," and conclude the Boutilier brothers were the murderers.

The Crown called fifteen witnesses, including three members of the Boutilier family. Stewart did not record how their testimony implicated their relatives. The most damning evidence came from Eminaud's son, who produced a broken piece of red chalk. On the afternoon before the killings, he explained, his father had broken the chalk in half as they worked. The chalk fragment was then compared to a piece of chalk found in George Boutilier's pocket when he was arrested. The two pieces fitted together perfectly. To round out the Crown's case, two men swore they saw the Boutilier brothers crossing the ice of a nearby waterway as they fled the scene of the crime.

No evidence was called by the defence, and Stewart does not record whether they even had a lawyer to defend them. Then it was Strange's turn to enter the spotlight with his instructions to the jury. "If you have the smallest doubt, whether it regard the fact of the murders, the fact of the prisoners having been at the house or the design and end with which they might have been there," he explained, "it is my duty to tell you, and yours to mind what I say, that you ought to acquit them." And the rationale was as relevant then as it is today: "It is better any number of guilty persons escape punishment than that one innocent man suffer."

But there was another option. "If you have no doubt," he continued, "but think that the finger of Providence has as plainly pointed the prisoners out doing this deed as if one had come and told you he saw them do it, in that case, and in that case only, you will find them guilty."

The chief justice then faced squarely the central issue of the trial — the prosecution's lack of direct evidence. "Wickedness often devises such secret times and ways to perpetrate its evil designs," he noted, "that if nothing but positive evidence could be received for juries to go upon in determining facts, crimes would forever go unpunished, and the condition of society [would] be rendered most insecure."

Circumstantial evidence, he contended, could be "even more conclusive than a simple testimony of the fact itself." He used the example of a man seen fleeing a house carrying a bloody knife. The only other occupant of the house was found stabbed to death. The implication of guilt was inescapable. Strange could have cited another compelling example — a piece of chalk belonging to a murder victim found in a suspect's pocket.

It took the jurors an hour and a half to return a verdict of guilty against each man. The murder of Eminaud was "so black and dreadful" it was "incapable of aggravation," the judge said in passing sentence. "Though from the present tribunal before which you stand you can receive nothing but strict and equal justice," he told the Boutiliers, "you are soon to appear before an almighty judge, whose unfathomable wisdom is able, by means incomprehensible to our narrow capacities, to reconcile justice with mercy." Strange encouraged the two to own up to their actions in the little time they had left. He ordered George and John Boutilier to hang within a week.

John Boutilier, the younger of the brothers, took the chief justice to heart and confessed his role in the murders to a clergyman. The sentence was carried out in Lunenburg on May 9, 1791, at a spot later dubbed Gallows Hill. "Their behaviour at the gallows was such as became men who were sensible of the horrid crime they had committed," one newspaper claimed. The Boutiliers were buried at Northwest, on the farm where they grew up.

Greed drove the Boutilier brothers to kill. It spurred them to steal everything in sight, even a piece of blood-red chalk — the shred of evidence that linked them beyond all doubt to the murders of the Eminauds.

Part Six

MURDER MOST FOUL

chapter 12

A Trust Betrayed

I t was the whisps of smoke, slowly rising into the morning air from a pile of brush, that first caught the attention of Isaiah Munro. Munro and his brothers had spent the morning cutting hay in an isolated meadow in the rugged country south of Annapolis Royal. Concerned the fire might spread, Munro wandered over to put it out. He later recalled that he "smelt meat burning" as he approached the smouldering brush, which covered a pile of stones.

It was then he made the grisly discovery that would fascinate and repulse an entire province.

"Before I got there I saw a bone sticking through the rocks ... and a foot sticking out." Horrified, he ran back and told his brothers before heading into Annapolis Royal, about ten miles away, to summon the coroner. An autopsy would later show the badly burned body was that of a woman in her thirties and five months pregnant. Although she had been struck on the head with a rock, she was still alive when set on fire. The Halifax *Morning Herald* hardly exaggerated when, borrowing from *Hamlet*, it reported the crime in its September 2, 1880 edition under a headline that screamed: "Murder Most Foul."

Suspicion immediately fell on a man seen driving a horse and wagon in the area only hours before the discovery. Locating that suspect became easy once the victim was identified as Charlotte Hill, an inmate of the poorhouse at North Range, a settlement a few miles south of Digby. Sheriff's deputies were immediately dispatched to find the keeper of the poorhouse, a prosperous farmer named Joseph Nick Thibault — or Tebo, as

129

the name was usually spelled by his anglophone neighbours. "He was a very shrewd, intelligent man" despite a lack of formal education, having amassed several thousand dollars "by skilful cattle trading and similar speculations," the author of a history of Annapolis County noted. As one of many sidelines to farming, the forty-five-year-old Thibault was paid $300 a year by the North Range district to look after paupers. Among them was Charlotte Hill.

Thibault was arrested September 3 at the North Range farm where he lived with his wife and children. A preliminary hearing was hastily convened at the courthouse in Annapolis Royal. Testifying before a courtroom described as "crowded to suffocation" with onlookers, poorhouse inmates confirmed that both Thibault and Hill had been missing from the farm on the night of August 31. Only Thibault had returned the following day. Fleshing out the picture, other witnesses told of seeing Thibault travelling with a female companion at sunrise on September 1 and later spotting him alone. Thibault pleaded not guilty to the charge of murder and was ordered to stand trial at the next sitting of the Supreme Court.

* * *

The trial of Joseph Thibault more than a century ago easily ranks among the most sensational in Nova Scotia history. Charlotte Hill's gruesome death, Thibault's position of trust as keeper of a poorhouse, and a personal prosecution by the attorney general all dictated that it would be no ordinary trial. The public was hungry for details of the heinous crime. An enterprising photographer who took a tintype of the dead woman's face sold about 100 copies before the trial. Press coverage was extensive. *The Morning Herald* dispatched a reporter from Halifax to file via telegraph lengthy, verbatim accounts of the often lurid evidence.

The trial opened December 1 at Annapolis Royal, which had the distinction of being the site of the first court of English common law in Canada, circa 1721. Presiding over the latest

John Thompson, a future prime minister, personally handled the prosecution of a poorhouse operator accused of murdering a woman in his care. (PANS/Photograph Collection)

chapter in the town's legal history was Mr. Justice Robert Weatherbe, forty-four, who was destined to become chief justice of Nova Scotia. The youngest man ever named to the Nova Scotia bench at the time of his appointment, he had served only two years when assigned the Thibault trial.

Underlining the seriousness of the case, Attorney General John S.D. Thompson chose to direct the prosecution in person. In those days the attorney general was expected to routinely handle cases in the Halifax courts. But prosecutions in the outlying counties usually fell to the most senior lawyer available — a tradition that often proved helpful to the defence. The case against Thibault, based totally on circumstantial evidence, was apparently judged too risky to leave in such uncertain hands.

Besides, Thompson probably relished the challenge. Only thirty-six, he had practised and taught law for fifteen years. He had been attorney-general for two years, a stepping stone to the future posts of premier, Supreme Court judge, federal minister of justice and, ultimately, prime minister of Canada. By 1880 he was considered the leading legal mind in the province. "Given his mastery of his material, his lucid mind, he became nearly invincible in court," wrote biographer Peter Waite. Thompson's task was to marshall the strands of weak evidence that would become a strong noose around Thibault's neck.

The prisoner was led into court and the trial began. Thibault "was closely shaven and coarsely dressed, wearing a striped guernsey, which suggested penitentiary garb," reported *The Morning Herald*. "He has lost much flesh during his imprisonment and has a haggard look." Thibault was defended by a trio of lawyers lead by Robert Motton, an experienced criminal defender imported from Halifax. After an unsuccessful defence attempt to challenge the entire jury panel as biased, twelve men were chosen to try the case.

Lawyer T.D. Ruggles, one of three lawyers assisting Thompson, opened the Crown's case, and laid it on thick. He stressed the "horrible character" of the murder and set the scene for the jurors, suggesting that Hill had been burned alive "while the fiendish author of the crime stood by and gloated over her agony." The coroner, Dr. Bungay, was called first to recite the condition of the body, rejecting a defence contention that the blow to the head could have been caused by a fall. Other witnesses who knew Hill, including a half-brother, identified her from the remains and a photograph. They described a woman in her mid-thirties hardened in appearance by a life of poverty — short with stooped shoulders, a thin face, and several missing front teeth.

The final witness of the first day was Addie Scott, Hill's friend and fellow inmate at Thibault's poorhouse. She responded to the prosecutor's questions with silence until the judge threatened to jail her for contempt. Even then, she refused to positively identify the prisoner as Thibault. "She's been tampered with," one onlooker suggested, prompting laughter from the spectators. To regain control of the courtroom, Weatherbe warned he would jail "at once" those responsible for further levity.

Scott proved no better a witness when her evidence continued the following day. But Thompson "was marvellously patient and gentle, and coaxed out of her, by degree, testimony about the inmates of the [poor]house, Tebo's horses, carriages," one reporter wrote admiringly. She told how Hill had gathered up her belongings in a borrowed basket before leaving the poorhouse the night of August 31. On cross-examination Scott was more forthcoming, telling the court that Hill had planned to run away. Thibault, she said, sometimes stayed overnight at another farm: "It was something for him to be home on a summer's night."

The Crown called a series of people who saw a wagon carrying a man and woman early on the morning of September 1. All described a man in dark hat and grey coat accompanied by a small woman, driving a dark horse and wagon. Within hours, they saw the man return in the opposite direction, alone and "driving fast." Although they identified the man as Thibault, Motton forced a few to admit on cross-examination that they could not be positive. But one man, Thomas Berry, testified he had known Thibault for about nine years. They had exchanged greetings as Thibault and the woman drove past.

The outdated system that had put Hill in Thibault's care came under fire during the trial. Thompson's assistant, Ruggles, criticized the "barbarous" practice, followed in some rural areas, of entrusting paupers to the lowest bidder. An official of the North Range poor district, John McNeil, testified that Thibault had held the contract for just over a year. When the witness said he did not know how many paupers had been in Thibault's care, Weatherbe became incensed. "That is extraordinary," the judge snapped. "If they had been sheep or cattle you would have had an accurate list."

* * *

By the trial's fourth day the Crown had only a few loose ends to tie up. Sheriff's deputies told of finding Thibault's horse and wagon hidden in the woods. The Munro brothers testified about finding the body. Thompson closed his case by calling Herbert Rhoddy, who was hauling lumber not far from the scene of the murder on October 18 when he spotted a partridge. Grabbing his gun, he chased the bird into a swamp and found a basket containing women's clothing and a photograph. The likeness was that of Charlotte Hill, the basket similar to one seen in Thibault's wagon the day of the crime.

The defence evidence was as brief as it was irrelevant. Motton called three witnesses, two simply to establish that members of Thibault's family had been subpoenaed by the Crown but did not testify. The third was a barber who shaved one of the prosecution's witnesses just before the trial. The man, he said, had bragged he was in town to "hang" Thibault. There was no effort to establish an alibi to counter the Crown's circumstantial case.

The next day, December 5, Motton began his closing remarks. The Crown, he asserted, was suggesting that "the prisoner had murdered the girl to cover up some shame and escape some expense," but "there was no evidence showing any improper relations" between Thibault and Hill. Motton charged that similarities in the evidence of many witnesses "showed that there had been some training somewhere" and he reminded the jurors of the "determined purpose in many minds to hang the prisoner." He finished by imploring them to acquit Thibault. "He was the bravest criminal ever known, if he were the man. Why had he travelled by daylight with the girl by his side? If he intended to murder her, would he have thus advertised the fact of his being in the girl's company?"

Thompson had an answer. "Men are never wise when they resort to crime," he said in his summation. "Innocence is the only wisdom." As for the danger of convicting an innocent man, he took the position that circumstantial evidence was persuasive. He used the example of a man seen entering a doctor's office and failing to emerge. The physician had been convicted of murder on the basis of a set of the man's false teeth, found among the ashes in a furnace. After reviewing testimony and the law for four hours, Thompson finished by contending it was not up to the Crown to suggest a motive. But, he added, "there are many men with fewer temptations to commit crime than Tebo had, and many women as defenceless as Charlotte Hill."

Thompson's lengthy speech delayed the judge's charge to the jury until the following day. "The criminal selects his own time and place for the deed," Weatherbe said of the Crown's lack of direct evidence. The jurors, he added, should consider the fact that Thibault could have proved his whereabouts at the time of the offence, but failed to do so. If they had a reasonable doubt of his guilt, however, they should acquit.

* * *

The jury retired at half-past one in the afternoon. Lawyers took advantage of the lull to dispose of bail hearings for two men charged with minor offences, but the wait was brief. "The stillness of death prevailed when at three o'clock the jury re-entered the courtroom," wrote the reporter for *The Morning Herald*, not missing a chance to add to the drama. But the verdict came as little surprise: guilty. All eyes turned to Thibault, who "sat like a statue," betraying no emotion until approached by his lawyer, Motton. "They have condemned an innocent man, sir," was Thibault's only response to the verdict.

The court reconvened on December 7. Asked if he had anything to say before sentence was passed, Thibault again protested his innocence. The murder, Weatherbe said, had been "attended by circumstances of brutality and cruelty .... God only

135

knows what were your motives." Then he pronounced sentence: death by hanging, to be carried out February 8, 1881. Thibault bowed his head and was led out of the courtroom.

Almost eight hundred people turned out for the execution, the first in Annapolis Royal in almost twenty years. The affair turned into a circus; the gallows in the jail yard was obscured by a twenty-foot-high wooden fence that was promptly torn down by an unruly mob eager for a public hanging. Guards reported that Thibault had paced the floor of his cell the previous night, but he appeared calm as he mounted the scaffold and the noose was fitted. The crowd fell silent as the trap gave way under Thibault's feet. Doctors declared him dead within minutes as spectators pressed forward for a better look.

Was Thibault guilty? Before the execution a story began circulating that Thibault had offered his version of events to friends. He had been taking Hill to another poorhouse on September 1 when they stopped for breakfast. Hill, who had threatened suicide in the past, suddenly threw herself into the fire. Unable to save her in time, Thibault panicked and covered the body with brush and rocks, fearing people would conclude he had killed her.

The explanation was far-fetched. The fact remained that Thibault was with Charlotte Hill before her death and was seen fleeing the scene. For a motive, one need look no further than Hill's pregnancy. Would a man in Thibault's position resort to murder to avoid the expense and embarrassment of an illegitimate child? There seems no other explanation for the brutal demise of Charlotte Hill.

chapter 13

Web of Lies

The sun was still hanging low in the morning sky when William Hussey approached the small, ramshackle cabin. It wasn't much, but this secluded farm near a river's mouth was home for John Clem. Hussey, his neighbour, had been promised some seed potatoes for spring planting, and he had come to collect.

It was still early, but Hussey thought it odd that the place looked deserted. After checking the barn, he climbed on the gunnel of a boat beached beside the cabin and peeked in a window. "I heard heavy groaning and I thought they were asleep," Hussey recalled.* Then a woman's voice broke the morning stillness, crying out: "Oh Lord, have mercy on us."

Startled, Hussey sprang from his perch and barged through the unbolted door. He was confronted by a sight he would not soon forget. "I saw Clem lying before the fire on his bed, on the broad of his back, with his hands crossed on his breast. He was senseless," he said later, when asked to describe the scene. "His eye was bruised and swollen and the pillow covered in blood."

Rushing to his side, Hussey shook Clem in an attempt to rouse him from his stupor. "I asked him who hurt him, but he made me no answer .... He snorted heavily and blood rushed from his mouth at every breath."

---

* At least that's the way *The Acadian Recorder* recounted Hussey's evidence at trial. The reporter for another Halifax newspaper, *The Novascotian*, was probably in error when he quoted Hussey as saying: "I heard a groaning — I thought it was a sheep."

Hussey moved on to the only other room in the cabin. There, lying amidst blood-spattered bedclothes, were Elizabeth Pipes, a widow who kept house for Clem, and her twelve-year-old daughter, Jane. "I thought they were dead," was Hussey's first reaction. But both were clinging to life, but neither could tell Hussey what had happened. The elder Pipes, her forehead battered and slashed open, muttered something about a "nightmare."

Hussey already had a suspect in mind. Suddenly, he looked up to see the shadow of a man against the wall. For a split second, he feared the assailant had returned to finish his handiwork. He spun around, but was relieved to find himself standing face to face with another neighbour, John Winsby. Winsby, who was dropping off a bag of barley, was just as relieved to see that it was Hussey kneeling over the mangled victims.

There was little they could do. Clem died within minutes. Beside his bed were the splintered remains of a wooden chest, in which the farmer was reputed to keep a large amount of cash; nothing of value remained. A bloodied axe would later be found just outside the cabin.

Hussey and Winsby had a good idea who had attacked the cabin's three occupants as they slept. Clem's hired hand, Maurice Doyle, was nowhere to be found. Leaving Hussey at the cabin to comfort the two left alive, Winsby went to the nearest town, Pugwash, to summon a doctor and spread word of what remains one of the most notorious murders in Nova Scotia history.

* * *

The date was June 28, 1838, and the citizens of Amherst were in a festive mood. It was the day of Queen Victoria's coronation, and her subjects in northern Nova Scotia's largest town were celebrating with parades and marching bands. But spirits dampened in the late afternoon when word arrived of the tragedy in River Phillip, about thirty miles due east. Rumours began to fly that the prime suspect in the murder, Doyle, had passed through

Amherst that morning on the way to neighbouring New Brunswick.

A two-man posse — more reminiscent of spaghetti westerns than pre-Confederation Nova Scotia — mounted up to give chase. The law was represented by Joseph Avard, a justice of the peace who carried the warrant for Doyle's arrest. His sidekick was Asa Filmore, a River Phillip resident who said he could identify their quarry.

After riding all night across the rough roads of backwoods New Brunswick, they pulled into the town of Sussex, a good 100 miles from Amherst. Doyle was about to board a stagecoach for Saint John when Filmore spotted him. Worried that Doyle might be armed, the pair took no chances. Filmore drew his pistol as Avard jumped Doyle and wrestled him to the ground. Caught off guard, Doyle offered no resistance as Avard tied him up with rope.

A search turned up a wallet containing £25 in bank notes, but no weapon. Told the reason for the arrest, Doyle seemed surprised.

"My God," he stammered. "Is Clem dead?"

"Yes," Filmore replied sternly, "and you are the supposed murderer and must return and answer."

They took their prisoner to the nearest tavern, no doubt to stock up on food and drink for the return trip to Amherst. Filmore, who was by now becoming something of a pro at this law-enforcement stuff, launched an impromptu interrogation. Asked where he got the money, Doyle said he earned the large sum through "hard labour" in the United States. To explain his hasty exit from River Phillip, Doyle told his captors he wanted to see his brother, who was about to sail from Saint John to the West Indies.

When the questions turned to Clem, Doyle praised his former employer as "a clever man." He "paid me well," Doyle said, but Clem told him on June 27 — the day before the murder — that his services were no longer needed. The last time he saw him, Doyle said, Clem was carrying a sack toward his farm and looking very much alive. Avard and Filmore didn't believe a word of it. Doyle was hauled back to Amherst, arraigned on a charge of murder, and tossed into jail to await a trial in the fall.

* * *

"The annals of crime contain few such midnight acts of atrocity," a newspaper writer with a flair for hyperbole proclaimed when Clem's murder hit the pages of Halifax's *Acadian Recorder*. Although initial reports held out little hope for the recovery of Pipes and her daughter, both survived their ordeal.

The task of prosecuting Doyle fell to James F. Gray, a Halifax lawyer with about a dozen years at the bar. His most notable case had come three years earlier — the high-profile but failed prosecution of outspoken Halifax editor Joseph Howe for criminal libel. At first glance, the Clem murder looked like a good chance for Gray to go zero for two. He had no eyewitnesses — the two survivors had no idea who had savagely attacked them in their sleep. But the circumstantial evidence pointing in Doyle's direction, coupled with his desperate attempt to flee, provided a good foundation for the Crown's case. The challenge for Gray was to collect enough scraps of evidence to put the axe that felled Clem firmly in Doyle's hands.

The show got under way on September 25, 1838, to a full house. "At an early hour of the morning the streets of Amherst were crowded with persons thronging in from the country to witness the trial," noted one observer on the scene. "It was with some difficulty that a passage for the chief justice and the officers of the court could be made through the mass of men at the door of the courthouse."

The judge who had to elbow his way into the courthouse was Brenton Halliburton. "A small, delicate, light complexioned man," in the words of one spectator, Halliburton hardly fit in among the broad-shouldered farmers and shipbuilders who called Amherst home. And he would have been just as happy to have remained in the cultured surroundings of Halifax — he confessed to friends that he loathed travelling around the countryside to conduct trials. A judge for half of his sixty-three years, he was in his fifth year as the colony's top judge. Of his legal knowledge, one lawyer who appeared before him offered the back-handed compliment that it "was not very extensive, but like his wine it was of the best quality."

With the judge on the bench, Gray called for the prisoner to be produced. Doyle was brought into the courtroom, manacled and surrounded by a bevy of guards carrying tip staves — a ceremonial, metal-tipped staff identifying them as sheriff's officers. On the chief justice's orders, the leg irons were removed once Doyle took his place in the prisoner's dock.

Doyle, only twenty-four, was a Cape Bretoner by birth who had taken odd jobs as a labourer in the River Phillip area for about a year before Clem's untimely death. He looked the part of a murderer, at least in the eyes of the newspaper reporters covering the trial. "A strong built, muscular man with large coarse features, dark hair and eyes, shaggy eyebrows and a down look," wrote the correspondent for the Halifax-based *Novascotian*. The whole package was a "mixture of brutality, ignorance and low cunning." *The Acadian Recorder*'s man in Amherst was equally uncharitable in his description of Doyle. "His visage is repulsive ... at least [it] contains nothing attractive." In an era when it was commonly believed that people who looked like criminals *were* criminals, Doyle's appearance alone may have been enough to convince a jury he was the killer.

A jury was chosen — the defence challenged only one of the thirteen men called forward — and the trial began. Gray rose to the occasion, laying out the prosecution's case in a lengthy, sometimes eloquent speech. He cautioned the jurors that even though details of the case had been widely circulated through the newspapers and the local rumour mill, "every feeling of excitement must be banished" from their minds. There could be no doubt this was a case of murder, not manslaughter — blows from an axe had rained down on three people as they slept, and one had died from his wounds. "Whoever committed the crime was, in law and in fact, a murderer," Gray asserted. The jury had only one issue to decide: Was Doyle that murderer?

"The testimony is but circumstantial," Gray continued, but that was understandable. "The man who meditates a murderous deed, chooses not the broad daylight for the perpetration of his crime; he seeks for darkness and secrecy — his steps are silent and unseen." But the prosecutor assured the jurors he could trace Doyle's movements for two crucial days, from the time of the offence to the sudden, supicious flight into the neighbouring colony. He would show that Doyle spun a web of lies to cover his tracks. And he would present the hard evidence needed to link Maurice Doyle to the brutal murder of John Clem.

* * *

Cumberland County's coroner, George Bayman, was the first of the prosecution's witnesses. He left little to the jury's imagination, presenting the axe, stained with dark patches of dried blood, found outside Clem's cabin. Hussey and Winsby followed, describing in grisly detail their discovery of the three victims. Winsby, apparently eager to explain what he was doing at Clem's cabin so early in the morning, recalled how Clem had stopped by the day before his death, June 27, exhausted from carrying a bag of barley several miles from Pugwash, the nearest village. Clem left the sack at Winsby's house and rowed across the river to his cabin. Winsby delivered the barley the next morning, only to find his friend near death.

When questioning was turned over to the defence, Doyle's lawyer did him no favours. Charles Halliburton was a young attorney who had been practising in Amherst for only two years. (Despite the identical surname, he was apparently not related to the chief justice.) As the trial unfolded, Halliburton's inexperience made itself painfully obvious. From Hussey, he elicited that Doyle had a reputation as "a drinking man." He did no better with Winsby. Under questioning from the defence lawyer, Winsby recalled that during his brief visit the day before his death, Clem had remarked that "Doyle was not faithful and he did not like him." Score two for the prosecution.

142

Samuel Patterson, a surgeon in Pugwash, performed the autopsy. Clem had died from a gaping wound to one temple that had penetrated two inches into the brain. Clem's head and shoulders were peppered with a number of other axe wounds, none of them fatal.

Gray now turned to proving Doyle had inflicted those wounds. His key witness was John Sentorius, who lived about two miles from Clem and made his living ferrying people across River Phillip. He described Doyle as "addicted to liquor," and recalled talking with the accused on June 27. Doyle had worked for Clem about three months, but said he had just been fired. Doyle borrowed a boat, and disappeared for about four hours. He returned the boat around midnight, and asked to be rowed to the other shore. After Doyle changed his shirt, Sentorius complied.

As they neared the spot where the road to Amherst met the river, Doyle made a strange request. If anyone asked, he implored Sentorius, say he had headed in the opposite direction, toward Pugwash. Sentorius was naturally suspicious, but Doyle explained he owed money and "he was going away because he could not pay it." That was not all — he had "deluded" a local farmer's daughter, and thought it best he move on.

"After a pause," Sentorius told the court, "he then said: 'all my dependence lies in you not telling which way I go'." With that, Doyle hopped out of the boat and disappeared into the darkness. Later, when he heard about Clem's murder, Sentorius checked the shirt Doyle had discarded in his kitchen. There was a speck of blood on each sleeve.

Halliburton, the defence lawyer, did what little he could to temper the damning evidence. Under cross-examination, Sentorius acknowledged that Doyle "did not appear worried" upon his return with the borrowed boat, "nor in a great hurry."

Another piece of the puzzle came from John Mulroy, who had a farm directly across the river from Clem's cabin. Doyle dropped in about ten o'clock on the night of June 27, and he was full of questions. Doyle's querries seemed "quite natural" at the time, Mulroy said, but in retrospect they took on a sinister air.

143

What time had Clem returned to his farm? Were Pipes' children there, or had they gone to their own home? Clem had returned about six, Doyle was told, and one of his housekeeper's daughters was staying the night. Doyle had no other business with the Mulroys, and left within half an hour.

The next person to see Doyle after Sentorius dropped him on the riverbank was George Glendenning. It was about dawn on June 28, and Doyle was walking on the main road about seven miles outside Amherst. He said his name was Hales, and gave Glendenning five shillings for a ride into town in his wagon, and five more to take him across the expanse of marshes to Sackville, a village just over the border in New Brunswick. As the wagon rattled over the dirt roads, Hales became talkative, saying he had run away from a ship docked at Pugwash. He was heading to Saint John to see his brother, who was also a sailor. Once they reached Sackville, Hales offered more money for a ride to the next village, but Glendenning declined. Asked to identify this fellow Hales, Glendenning pointed across the courtroom to Doyle.

Avard and Filmore, the two-man police force, recounted their pursuit and capture of Doyle for the jury's benefit. Besides the wallet containing a large sum of money, their search of Doyle's pockets turned up two papers that looked suspicious. The prosecutor, Gray, called Pugwash merchant Henry Pineo to the witness stand to explain their significance. Pineo testified he had Doyle arrested in the spring for failing to pay thirty-two shillings owing for goods, but Clem had assumed the debt when he took on Doyle as a labourer. Shown the first paper, Pineo said it was an account of that transaction. That might be a legitimate item for Doyle to have in his possession, but the other paper was not. Pineo said it detailed a year-old transaction between himself and Clem that had nothing to do with Doyle.

Gray now zeroed in on the wallet. Abraham Seaman told the court he had repaired a wallet for Clem about eight years earlier, using a black strap because he had no red leather to match. Shown the wallet taken from Doyle, Seaman immediately recognized his handiwork.

Elizabeth Pipes, the woman left for dead, put the final nail in Doyle's coffin. Still bearing the scars of the attack, she testified that Clem had gone to Pugwash with Doyle on June 27 to settle accounts. Clem returned alone about six in the evening, and went to bed early. Pipes and her daughter went to sleep in the other room. Her next memory was speaking to a doctor several days later. Pipes said Clem carried his money and papers in a wallet and stored it in a wooden chest at the head of his bed. A few days before his death, she counted out £40 in banknotes. "That's the book," she exclaimed when Gray showed her the black and red wallet, "there's no mistake about it."

Halliburton went fishing for character evidence when it came his turn to question Pipes. She agreed with the defence lawyer's suggestion that Doyle was not a malicious man. Then she dropped a bombshell, recalling an instance when Doyle had threatened to "cut my damned head off when he would catch me alone."

* * *

Given Halliburton's poor track record with the prosecution's witnesses, it was probably best that he chose to call no defence witnesses. Doyle himself had no right to testify — allowing an accused to give evidence in a criminal trial was forbidden until almost the turn of the century in Canada. But defendants had the right to make a statement to the jury, which was of course taken with a grain of salt because it was not testimony given under oath. Offered a chance to make a statement, Doyle disputed the evidence of only one witness, Pipes. "She never saw that pocketbook before it was taken from me," he insisted. "It belongs to me."

Chief Justice Halliburton canvassed all the testimony and left the jurors no doubt where he stood. "It is my duty to tell you that these circumstances weigh most strongly against the prisoner," he said as he closed his instructions to the jury. "The night before the murder the property is in Clem's house, and 10 o'clock the same night the prisoner is within half a mile of the house. On Friday morning he is 120 miles off, with the property on him. In the name of God how got he the property? If he is not the person who committed the deed, how came he by the property?"

The jurors filed out to deliberate. It didn't take long — ten minutes according to *The Novascotian*'s reporter, twenty if you believe *The Acadian Recorder*. Either way, the verdict was guilty of murder. "The prisoner, who appeared to have entertained hopes of acquittal to the last, sunk on hearing the verdict. He buried his face in his hands," wrote one of the newsmen of Doyle's reaction. "It was a melancholy spectacle," agreed the other, "and it strengthened one in the opinion that the prisoner had entertained the belief that he could not be convicted of the homicide upon circumstantial testimony and presumption."

Doyle continued to sob as the judge sentenced him to die on the gallows in two days. "Never, in the course of a long professional life, have I met with an instance of depravity equal to that with which you now stand convicted," the chief justice intoned. "To the surrounding multitude ... let the fate of this unhappy man be a lesson." Doyle's temptation had been "to possess himself solely of the property of another, and that very property which formed the temptation has been the chief means of his detection."

The trial and execution of Doyle, *The Novascotian* editorialized, "afforded a striking exemplification of the strength which circumstantial evidence occasionally assumes." Doyle had the motive and opportunity to commit murder. The red wallet with the black strap, a damning piece of evidence he could have easily tossed by the wayside, sealed his fate.

chapter 14

Murdered Promise

On a March evening in 1915, Harry Allen pulled a .22-calibre pistol from his pocket, walked into the dining room of his sister's house, and gunned down the most prominent member of Nova Scotia's black community. That senseless act not only claimed the life of James Robinson Johnston, the province's first black lawyer; it also snuffed out the promise of what could have been.

Johnston, only the third Canadian-born black to earn a law degree, was only thirty-nine at the time of his murder. But he had already emerged as the most respected black leader of his day. Active in the Baptist church and the Conservative party, he was a strong advocate of equal educational opportunities for blacks. "In Mr. Johnston's death," *The Halifax Herald* lamented, "Halifax has lost a good citizen, the bar of Nova Scotia has lost a lawyer who was an ornament in it, and in every respect the city is the poorer." Johnston was the only Nova Scotia lawyer ever to be murdered, and his funeral drew some 10,000 people, white and black. Even Prime Minister Robert Borden, himself a former Halifax lawyer, sent a telegram expressing his condolences.

But Johnston's legacy died with him on March 3, 1915. It would be four decades before another Nova Scotia-born black followed in his footsteps and entered the legal profession. In death, Johnston "simply did not have the level or degree of significance that one would expect from someone who was so influential in his life," noted Barry Cahill, a Halifax historian who has exhaustively researched Johnston's short career. Cahill goes so far as to dub Johnston "the Martin Luther King of Nova

Scotia," noting similarities with the American civil rights leader. But unlike King, who became a martyr after he was killed by an assassin's bullet in 1968, Johnston's premature death only hastened his descent into obscurity.

Allen, his killer, was the brother of Johnston's wife and a boarder in their home. At trial, Allen's defence was an all-out effort, based on rather flimsy evidence, to sully Johnston's name and paint him as an abusive husband. The gambit failed to keep Allen out of prison, but it tarnished Johnston's reputation for generations. As Cahill put it, "a shadow was cast that caused him to be consigned to oblivion for a long time."

* * *

The grandson of a preacher, James Robinson Johnston was born in Halifax in 1876. His scholastic abilities allowed him to break free of the city's racially segregated schools and at age sixteen he became the first Nova Scotia-born black to study at Halifax's Dalhousie University. Six years later he scored another first when he graduated from Dalhousie's law school. Johnston described his admission to the bar on July 18, 1900, as "a red letter day in my life."

He quickly established himself as a specialist in military and criminal law, acting on behalf of blacks and whites alike. In one high-profile case in March 1914, Johnston used skilful cross-examination to win an acquittal for James Murphy, a penniless Irishman accused of a brutal murder. No lesser authority than the trial judge praised Johnston's impassioned address to the jury as "decidedly clever, ingenious and well-delivered."

Active in church affairs, Johnston also took a keen interest in education, which had been his own ticket to a better life. He was an early promoter of a vocational training school for blacks, but he did not live to see that dream realized with the opening of the Nova Scotia Home for Coloured Children in 1921. "He was not a scholar, he was very much a professional man. He saw education as a means to an end, not an end in itself," Cahill says. "He laid great stress on education. From his own early life he was very concerned with the formation of black youth .... He saw himself as a role model."

The oratorical skills that served Johnston so well in the courtroom benefited the Conservative party on the hustings. Johnston helped deliver Halifax's black vote to the Tories, and was emerging as a possible candidate for elected office in his own right. There was talk that he might run for an alderman's post in the Halifax civic election slated for the spring of 1915.

But that talk ended on March 3. After working at his downtown law office, Johnston returned at his two-storey frame home in the city's north end about six o'clock. Johnston, his wife of thirteen years, Jennie, and her younger brother, Harry Allen, ate supper together. Allen had been boarding with the Johnstons for four months, and Johnston had helped him land a job looking after horses being shipped overseas for the war effort. The meal passed without incident, but tensions were building below the surface.

Allen and his sister had had a spat about a month earlier, after the Johnstons returned from a trip to the United States. Jennie Johnston had accused Allen of having his girlfriend stay at the house during their absence, and the argument had become so heated that her husband had been forced to intervene. "Mr. Johnston said he [Allen] should not talk to me like that," she recalled later, admitting the two men "did not like each other."

After supper, Johnston remained at the dinner table, playing solitaire, while his wife cleaned up in the kitchen. Allen went upstairs, fetched a revolver from his dresser, and entered the dining room. "My God, Harry, don't shoot me!" Johnston cried as gunshots rang out.

Allen, the only eyewitness to his crime, has to be taken at his word in describing what happened. Testifying in his own defence at trial, Allen claimed that Johnston stuck out his tongue at him when he entered the room. Replying in kind, Allen thumbed his nose. "Is that so?" he quoted Johnston as saying as he grabbed a chair and approached his brother-in-law. Allen, insisting he acted in self-defence, pulled the gun from his pocket

James Robinson Johnston, Nova Scotia's first black lawyer and a promising community leader, was cut down in the prime of his life by a murderer's bullet. (Dalhousie University)

and squeezed off four shots. Three bullets hit Johnston in the head; powder burns around the wounds suggested the gun was fired at point-blank range.

Bleeding from his wounds, Johnston was still able to chase Allen outside. They scuffled on the lawn of the house next door before Allen fired a fourth bullet into Johnston's head, killing him. A neighbour finally tackled Allen, who was in such a fit of rage that he was strangling the corpse.

Allen fled the scene before the police and coroner arrived, but was back within the hour. "I am the man you are looking for," he announced to Detective Frank Hanrahan. Later, on the way to the police station, Allen was told Johnston was dead. "My God," he said. "What have I done? What has come over me?"

Allen's confession made his murder conviction seem a foregone conclusion. But Johnston's widow saw that her brother had a lawyer, retaining a transplanted Englishman named James Terrell. Terrell's strategy was simple: put the victim on trial. Johnston had had a temper, and the defence exploited it in a bid to save Allen from the gallows. Jennie Johnston, who had lost her husband and faced the strong possibility of losing her brother, was the key figure in Terrell's exercise in posthumous character assassination.

Allen stood trial twice. He was convicted in late March, 1915, but a new trial was ordered because it had not been properly explained to the jury that evidence of provocation could reduce a charge of murder to manslaughter. The only hint of provocation was the suggestion that Allen was angered by the way Johnston treated his sister. Jennie Johnston's testimony on that point grew darker each time she took the witness stand. At the preliminary hearing she acknowledged having had arguments with her husband; by the time of the second trial in the fall of 1915, she told Terrell that Johnston had hit her and had threatened to kill her "several times."

Despite the defence tactic, Allen was convicted a second time. He was sentenced to hang but on New Year's Eve, 1915, the federal government commuted the sentence to life in prison. Allen served fourteen years before being paroled in 1929. By the time Allen died in Toronto in 1935, Johnston's life and death were little more than a bad memory.

*   *   *

Johnston's formidable accomplishments in his short life magnify the senselessness of his death. "If he had lived the normal span," says Cahill, "one can only speculate on how different the subsequent history of the [black] community in Nova Scotia might have been."

With his political connections, Johnston could well have become Nova Scotia's first black judge. That milestone was not reached until the 1980s. Had he chosen politics, he would have been a strong candidate for municipal office, predating the election of Halifax's first black alderman by sixty years. And it follows that Johnston could have made the jump to provincial politics. More than three quarters of a century after his murder, in the spring of 1993, a black was finally elected to the Nova Scotia legislature.

But Johnston's memory and achievements have been resurrected through the establishment of a chair in Black Studies at his alma mater, Dalhousie University. Beginning with the appointment of the first professor in 1994, the chair eventually will create a nucleus of black scholars in a variety of disciplines. When it came to naming the chair, Johnston was the logical choice. "Seventy-five years later," noted Cahill, "he's perhaps on the verge of being rehabilitated."